KU-691-549

A Stocking Full of Christmas

The Ultimate Collection of Festive Gems

Mark Stibbe

MONARCH
BOOKS

Oxford, UK & Grand Rapids, Michigan, USA

Copyright © Mark Stibbe 2005.
The right of Mark Stibbe to be identified
as author of this work has been asserted by him in
accordance with the Copyright, Designs
and Patents Act 1988.

All rights reserved.
No part of this publication may be reproduced or
transmitted in any form or by any means, electronic
or mechanical, including photocopying, recording or any
information storage and retrieval system, without
permission in writing from the publisher.

First published in the UK in 2005 by Monarch Books
(a publishing imprint of Lion Hudson plc),
Mayfield House, 256 Banbury Road, Oxford, OX2 7DH.
Tel: +44 (0) 1865 302750   Fax: +44 (0) 1865 302757
Email: monarch@lionhudson.com
www.lionhudson.com

ISBN-13: 978-1-85424-723-0 (UK)
ISBN-10: 1-85424-723-9 (UK)
ISBN-13: 978-1-0 8254-6089-0 (USA)
ISBN-10: 0-8254-6089-1 (USA)

Distributed by:
UK: Marston Book Services Ltd, PO Box 269,
Abingdon, Oxon OX14 4YN;
USA: Kregel Publications, PO Box 2607,
Grand Rapids, Michigan 49501.

Unless otherwise stated, Scripture quotations are taken from the Holy Bible, New International
Version, © 1973, 1978, 1984 by the International Bible Society.
Used by permission of Hodder and Stoughton Ltd. All rights reserved. All remaining quotations
are taken from the English Standard Version of the Bible, published by HarperCollins Publishers,
© 2001 by Crossway Books, a division of Good News Publishers.
Used by permission. All rights reserved.

British Library Cataloguing Data
A catalogue record for this book is available
from the British Library.

Book design and production for the publishers by Lion Hudson plc.
Printed in Malta.

FOREWORD

The Christmas season is my favourite time of the year and Mark Stibbe's *A Stocking Full of Christmas* is truly a festive gem – filled with a bountiful content of creativity.

As I read through the manuscript I found myself in deep reflection as stories and quotes illuminated my thinking, touched my heart and made me smile and laugh.

This book will bring Christmas cheer to all the family – you will be surprised and amused.

A Stocking Full of Christmas is filled with insights that reveal the essence and the promise of the season. Mark Stibbe reminds me of profound truths and the poignant quotes and straplines help me to remember them. Just as the best stories bear repeating time after time, you will want to unwrap this festive gem, year after year, and quote it to others.

Peace Be With You this Christmastime.
J. John

A is for Angels

That night some shepherds were in the fields outside the village, guarding their flocks of sheep. Suddenly, an angel of the Lord appeared among them, and the radiance of the Lord's glory surrounded them. They were terribly frightened, but the angel reassured them. "Don't be afraid!" he said. (Luke 2:8–10)

There are angels everywhere in the Christmas story. An angel turns up and informs Zechariah that his elderly wife is going to have a baby boy (later to become John the Baptist). An angel turns up and tells Mary that the Holy Spirit is going to overshadow her and she's going to give birth to the Son of God. An angel turns up and tells Joseph, Mary's husband-to-be, that his fiancée is pregnant as a result of the Holy Spirit and that he is to go ahead and marry her. An angel turns up and tells the shepherds watching their flocks that a Saviour has been born in the little town of Bethlehem. (This is followed by a choir of angels singing glory to God.) Everywhere you look in the story of Christ's birth, angels are found playing a critical role.

Music is well said to be the speech of angels: in fact, nothing among the utterances allowed to man is felt to be so divine. It brings us near to the infinite.

Thomas Carlyle

Whenever angels appear in the Christmas story they never fail to say "don't be afraid". In fact, this happens four times during the events of the birth of Jesus. Someone has counted the number of times we read "don't be afraid" in the Bible. It amounts to 365. That's one for each day of the year. God does not want us to live in fear.

It is superstitious to worship angels; it is proper to love them. Although it would be a high sin, and an act of misdemeanour against the Sovereign Court of Heaven to pay the slightest adoration to the mightiest angel, yet it would be unkind and unseemly, if we did not give to holy angels a place in our heart's warmest love.

Charles Spurgeon, Christmas sermon, delivered on 20 December 1857 at the Music Hall, Royal Surrey Gardens.

Whether the angels play only Bach in praising God I am not quite sure; I am sure however that all together they play Mozart.

Karl Barth

In September 1960, I woke up one morning with six hungry babies and just 75 cents in my pocket. Their father was gone. The boys ranged from three months to seven years; their sister was two. Their dad had never been much more than a presence they feared. Whenever they heard his tyres crunch on the gravel driveway they would scramble to hide under their beds. He did manage to leave $15 a week to buy groceries. Now that he had decided to leave there would be no more beatings, but no food either.

If there was a welfare system in effect in southern Indiana at that time, I certainly knew nothing about it. I scrubbed the kids until they looked brand new and then put on my best home-made dress. I loaded them into the rusty old car and drove off to find a job. The seven of us went to every factory, store and restaurant in our small town. No luck. The kids stayed crammed into the car and tried to be quiet while I tried to convince whoever would listen that I was willing to learn or do anything. I had to have a job. Still no luck.

The last place we went to, just a few miles out of town, was an old drive-in that had been converted into a truck stop. It was called the Big Wheel. An old lady named Granny owned the place, and she peeked out of the window from time to time at all those kids. She needed someone on the graveyard shift, eleven at night until seven in the morning. She paid 65 cents an hour and I could start that night. I raced home and called the teenager down the street who babysat for people. I bargained with her to come and sleep on my sofa for a dollar a night. She could arrive with her pyjamas on and the kids would already be asleep. This seemed like a good arrangement to her, so we made a deal.

That night when the little ones and I knelt to say our prayers we all thanked God for finding Mummy a job. And so I started at the Big Wheel.

When I got home in the mornings I woke the babysitter up and sent her home with one dollar of my tip money – fully half of what I averaged every night. As the weeks went by, heating bills added a strain to my meagre wage. The tyres on the old car had the consistency of penny balloons and began to leak. I had to fill them with air on the way to work and again every morning before I could go home.

One bleak autumn morning, I dragged myself to the car to go home and found four tyres on the back seat. New tyres! There was no note, no anything, just those beautiful brand new tyres. Had angels taken up residence in Indiana, I wondered.

I made a deal with the local service station. In exchange for his mounting the new tyres, I would clean up his office. I remember it took me a lot longer to scrub his floor than it did for him to do the tyres.

I was now working six nights instead of five and it still wasn't enough. Christmas was coming and I knew there would be no money for toys for the kids. I found a can of red paint and started repairing and painting some old toys. Then I hid them in the basement so there would be something for Santa to deliver on Christmas morning. Clothes were a worry too. I was sewing patches on top of patches on the boys' trousers, and soon they would be too far gone to repair.

On Christmas Eve the usual customers were drinking coffee in the Big Wheel. These were the truckers, Les, Frank and Jim, and a state trooper named Joe. A few musicians were hanging around after a gig at the Legion and dropping nickels into the pinball machine. The regulars all just sat around and talked until the wee hours of the morning, and then left to get home before the sun came up.

When it was time for me to go home at seven o'clock on Christmas morning, I hurried to the car. I was hoping the kids wouldn't wake up before I had managed to get home, get the presents from the basement and place them under the tree. (We had cut down a small cedar tree by the side of the road down by the dump.)

It was still dark and I couldn't see much, but there appeared to be some dark shadows in the car – or was that just a trick of the night? Something certainly looked different, but it was hard to tell what.

When I reached the car I peered warily through one of the side windows. Then my jaw dropped in amazement. My old battered car was filled to the top with boxes of all shapes and sizes. I quickly opened the driver's door, scrambled inside and knelt in the front facing the back seat.

Reaching back, I pulled off the lid of the top box. Inside was whole case of little blue jeans, sizes 2–10! I looked inside another box: it was full of shirts to go with the jeans. Then I peeked inside some of the other boxes: there were sweets and nuts and bananas and bags of groceries. There was an enormous ham for baking, and canned vegetables and potatoes. There was pudding and jelly and biscuits, pie filling and flour. There was a whole bag of laundry supplies and cleaning items. And there were five toy trucks and one beautiful little doll.

As I drove back through empty streets while the sun slowly rose on most amazing Christmas Day of my life, I was sobbing with gratitude. And I will never forget the joy on the faces of my little ones that precious morning.

Yes, there were angels in Indiana that long-ago December. And they all hung out at the Big Wheel truck stop.

At one school, two little girls were talking about their roles in the nativity play. "I'm going to be a virgin," one announced smugly.

"That's nothing," replied the other, "I'm going to be an angel."

"Well my mummy says it's much harder to be a virgin," retorted the first.

The world has angels all too few, And heaven is overflowing.

Coleridge

"We shall find peace. We shall hear angels. We shall see the sky sparkling with diamonds."

Anton Chekov

Mothers and angels often come together in the Bible. Sarah, Hagar, Elizabeth and Mary all have this in common. Their delivery is announced by an angel of God. And with each delivery comes not only a child but also a promise of deliverance. Throughout the Bible, it is these two messages that God's messengers bring: delivery and deliverance. "Behold, you will be delivered of a child," and "Behold, you will be delivered from oppression."

First delivery, then deliverance.

Off to one side sits a group of shepherds. They sit silently on the floor, perhaps perplexed, perhaps in awe, no doubt in amazement. Their night watch had been interrupted by an explosion of light from heaven and a symphony of angels. God goes to those who have time to hear him – and so on this cloudless night he went to simple shepherds.

Max Lucado

While shepherds watched their flocks
by night,
All seated on the ground,
The angel of the Lord came down,
And glory shone around,
And glory·shone around.

"Fear not!" said he, for mighty dread
Had seized their troubled minds.
"Glad tidings of great joy I bring
To you and all mankind,
To you and all mankind."

B is for Bethlehem

But you, O Bethlehem Ephrathah, are only a small village in Judah. Yet a ruler of Israel will come from you, one whose origins are from the distant past. (Micah 5:2)

Bethlehem (which means "House of Bread") is a small town six miles south-west of Jerusalem, nearly 2,500 feet above sea level. Its population was not great at the time of Jesus. In Old Testament times David lived in Bethlehem until he was anointed by the prophet Samuel to be king. David was a shepherd in his youth on the hills surrounding this small town. After King David's time Bethlehem faded into insignificance. Only the prophet Micah seems to have foreseen that this town would one day be the venue for the most important birth in human history. An inn in Bethlehem was therefore an unlikely place for the birth of God's Son. As Dan Schaeffer notes, "A Bethlehem inn was no Holiday Inn. It was a crude series of stalls built inside an enclosure, with a fire pit for cooking". But appearances can be deceptive.

In 1858 a scientific expedition passed through the part of America known as the Grand Canyon. A young lieutenant made this entry in his report:

"This region ... is ... altogether valueless. It can be approached only from the south, and after leaving it, there is nothing to do but leave. It ... shall be forever unvisited and undisturbed."

Today the Grand Canyon is one of the most visited places in the USA!

Christmas in Bethlehem. The ancient dream: a cold, clear night made brilliant by a glorious star, the smell of incense, shepherds and wise men falling to their knees in adoration of the sweet baby, the incarnation of perfect love.
Lucinda Franks

In 1865, a young American called Phillips Brooks journeyed on horseback from Jerusalem to Bethlehem. At the end of his journey he attended a Christmas Eve service in the Church of the Nativity in Bethlehem. Three years later, Brooks returned to America, but the memory of the land of Jesus remained very vivid within his heart. At the age of 32, Brooks used these powerful memories as the basis for writing his famous carol, "O Little Town of Bethlehem". At the time he was rector of the Church of the Advent and Holy Trinity Church in Philadelphia. He wrote the hymn for the children of his Sunday School. But after his organist, Lewis Redner, had put the words to the tune we know today, the carol became one of the most beloved of all Christmas hymns. Phillips Brooks was later to become the Bishop of Massachusetts, but he is remembered most of all for the inspired words of the carol "O Little Town of Bethlehem".

A Christmas Creed

I believe in Jesus Christ and in the beauty of the gospel begun in Bethlehem.

I believe in the one whose spirit glorified a little town; and whose spirit still brings music to persons all over the world, in towns both large and small.

I believe in the one for whom the crowded inn could find no room, and I confess that my heart still sometimes wants to exclude Christ from my life today.

I believe in the one whom the rulers of the earth ignored and the proud could never understand; whose life was among common people, whose welcome came from persons of hungry hearts.

I believe in the one who proclaimed the love of God to be invincible.

I believe in the one whose cradle was a mother's arms, whose modest home in Nazareth had love as its only wealth, who looked at persons and made them see what God's love saw in them, who by love brought sinners back to purity, and lifted human weakness up to meet the strength of God.

The hinge of history is to be found on the door of a Bethlehem stable.
Ralph W Sockman

I confess my everlasting need of God: the need for forgiveness for our selfishness and greed; the need for new life for empty souls; the need for love for hearts grown cold.

I believe in God who gives us the best of himself. I believe in Jesus, the son of the living God, born in Bethlehem this night, for me and for the world.

Anonymous

And so the incredible paradox of all happened at Bethlehem: History's greatest figure was born, not in a palace or a mansion, but in a cavern-stable.

Paul Maier

Take time to be aware that in the very midst of our busy preparations for the celebration of Christ's birth in ancient Bethlehem, Christ is reborn in the Bethlehems of our homes and daily lives. Take time, slow down, be still, be awake to the Divine Mystery that looks so common and so ordinary and yet is wondrously present.

Edward Hays

It is interesting to reflect on how it was that Jesus came to be born in Bethlehem, in fulfilment of Old Testament prophecy. After all, his birthplace should have been Nazareth, the home of his parents, Joseph and Mary. However, the Roman Emperor, Caesar Augustus, issued a census edict and all his subjects throughout the vast empire had to return to their ancestral homes to enrol. For Joseph and Mary this meant making the 80-mile trip from Nazareth to Bethlehem, a journey that would have taken them five to six days.

This edict had two important consequences. It first of all took Mary away from Nazareth and the embarrassment of her pregnancy becoming increasingly obvious.

Secondly, it meant that Jesus was born in Bethlehem, in fulfilment of what the prophet Micah had foreseen. With such ordinary events God works out his extraordinary purposes.

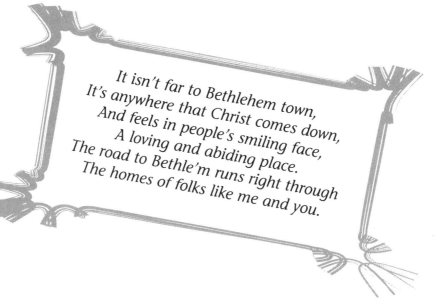

It isn't far to Bethlehem town,
It's anywhere that Christ comes down,
And feels in people's smiling face,
A loving and abiding place.
The road to Bethle'm runs right through
The homes of folks like me and you.

A very religious couple was touring the Holy Land during the Christmas season and decided that it would be very meaningful to them to spend Christmas Eve in Bethlehem, the birthplace of Jesus. Arriving there, they searched high and low for a room, but none was available at any price. Finally, they pulled up in front of the Sheraton-Bethlehem and the husband got out of the car, telling his wife: "Stay here, sweetie. Let me see if I can do something for us."

He approached the desk and the receptionist told him there were no rooms. "Sorry, sir. It's Christmas Eve, our busiest time."

No matter how much the man offered to pay, the receptionist said he had nothing. Finally, the man told the receptionist: "I bet if I told you my name was Joseph, that the woman waiting in the car was called Mary, and that she had a newborn infant, you'd find us a room."

"Well," stammered the receptionist, "I – I suppose so."

"Okay," said the man. "I guarantee you they're not coming tonight, so we'll take their room."

O little town of Bethlehem,
How still we see thee lie!
Above thy deep and dreamless sleep
The silent stars go by;
Yet in thy dark streets shineth
The everlasting Light;
The hopes and fears of all the years
Are met in thee tonight.

C is for Carols

Suddenly, the angel was joined by a vast host of others – the armies of heaven – praising God: "Glory to God in the highest heaven, and peace on earth to all whom God favours." (Luke 2:13–14)

The chorus of angels praising God was the first ever Christmas carol. We don't know what the melody was or how many different parts there were in the arrangement. We don't know how many voices sang, or whether those voices were male, female, or both. All we do know is that the lyrics of this carol spanned the vast vistas of both heaven and earth. On the one hand the angels' words pointed to the glory of God in the highest heavens. On the other, they pointed to our greatest need here on the earth – peace on our planet. The carol may be brief in duration but it is massive in its scope. It is an abiding reminder that something doesn't have to be eternal in order to be immortal.

Carols were first sung in Europe before the time of Christianity. These were pagan songs sung at the winter solstice celebration. The word carol means dance or song of joy. Carols used to be composed and used at all times of the year, but only the tradition of singing them at Christmas survived! The early church replaced the solstice celebrations with Christmas and devised Christian songs to sing instead. In AD 129, a Roman bishop decreed that the song "Angel's Hymn" should be sung at a Christmas service in Rome. This is one of the first Christmas carols known to us.

A British clergyman struggled along with a small congregation in a small community. A commercial firm offered to supply free hymn books, provided they could insert a bit of discreet advertising into the hymnals. The pastor was reluctant but finally agreed. When the hymnals arrived, he eagerly examined them and was delighted to find no brash advertisements on or inside the covers. The next Sunday, his flock began to sing from the hymnals. All went well until the third song, in which the congregation lifted their voices in unison to the melodious notes of:

Hark the herald angels sing,
Hanson's pills are just the thing;
Peace on earth and mercy mild,
Two for men and one for child.

One night Freda went carol-singing.

She knocked on the door of a house and began to sing. A man with a violin in his hand came to the door.

Within half a minute tears were streaming down his face! Freda went on singing for half an hour, every carol she knew – and some she didn't.

As last she stopped.

"I understand," she said softly. "You are remembering your happy childhood Christmas days. You're a sentimentalist!"

"No," he snivelled. "I'm a musician!"

"Away in a Manger" is the best-known and best-loved Christmas carol, according to a survey published in December 2003. Two-thirds of those polled said they knew all the words of the carol and more than 7 out of 10 said they attended a carol service every year. "Silent Night" and "O Little Town of Bethlehem" were second and third respectively.

In a question about which person was most associated with Christmas, the same poll had Cliff Richard in fourth place and the Vicar of Dibley in tenth. They were the only people who had any kind of association with Christianity in the top ten answers. The Trotter family came first (from *Only Fools and Horses*) and Morecambe and Wise second.

"What would you like for a Christmas present?" For any young girl, such a question would evoke delighted visions of long-wished-for possessions, but for Dolly the answer to her father, John Byron, was, "Please write me a poem". So on Christmas morning in 1749, Dolly found on her plate at breakfast a piece of paper on which was written a hymn entitled "Christmas day, for Dolly".

Soon after, John Wainwright, the organist of Manchester Parish Church, wrote a tune for it. On the following Christmas morning, Byron and Dolly were awakened by the sound of singing below their windows. It was Wainwright with his choir, singing Dolly's hymn, "Christians, Awake".

A little boy and girl were singing their favourite Christmas carol, "Silent Night". The boy concluded the rendition with the words, "Sleep in heavenly beans". His sister quickly corrected him: "It's not beans, it's peas."

Christians, awake, salute the happy
    morn,
Whereon the Saviour of the world was
    born;
Rise to adore the mystery of love,
Which hosts of angels chanted from
    above;
With them the joyful tiding first begun
Of God incarnate and the Virgin's Son.

I heard the bells on Christmas Day
Their old familiar carols play
And mild and sweet the words repeat,
Of peace on earth, goodwill to men.

D is for Decorations

After this interview the wise men went their way. Once again the star appeared to them, guiding them to Bethlehem. It went ahead of them and stopped over the place where the child was. When they saw the star, they were filled with joy! (Matthew 2:9–10)

The first ever Christmas decoration was the star that led the wise men to Bethlehem, birthplace of the Messiah. This light illuminated the night sky and pointed the way to the stable where Jesus lay. People are divided about whether this star was a natural or a supernatural phenomenon. Some argue that this was a conjunction of Jupiter, Saturn and Mars in 6 BC, or Halley's comet (12 BC), or another comet (known as comet no. 52) in 5 BC, or a nova (one that appeared in 4 BC). Others argue that this light was the radiant glory of the Lord. Either way, the star of Bethlehem has been the inspiration behind at least some of the decorations that we see at Christmas, particularly Christmas-tree lights and candles. In nations such as Norway, where the nights are darker and longer in the winter, Christmas lights are particularly important.

Perhaps the best Yuletide decoration is being wreathed in smiles.

I read about a Christmas play where the little children dressed up like shepherds, wise men, angels and other characters of Christmas.

The highlight of the Christmas play was to show the radiance of Jesus. An electric bulb was hidden in the manger. All the stage lights were to be turned off, leaving only one light in the manger.

At the appropriate time, all lights went out.

Even the manger light.

The silence was broken when one of the little shepherds loudly whispered,

"Hey, you turned off Jesus."

In the 1890s a young boy in America fell ill and was confined to his bed during the winter months. All he could see from his window was a large evergreen tree. To cheer himself up, he asked his father to drape lights over the tree. His father, the owner of an electrical business, put coloured lights all over the tree and his son watched them glow and sparkle like jewels against the white cloak of snow. People heard about  these lights and came in horse-drawn carriages from miles away to see the extraordinary sight. By 1895 illuminated Christmas trees had appeared all over America and spread even further afield.

Today, Christmas trees the world over are lit up by brightly coloured lights to remind everyone that the light shines in the darkness and the darkness cannot overcome it (John 1:5).

There once was a shining Christmas tree
Standing out where all could see.
Its brilliance captured every eye
And seemed to cheer each passer-by.

"The lights are so bright," they would say
And hesitate to walk away.
The tree stood proud ablaze with light
For every light was burning bright.

Then one bulb was heard to say
"I'm tired of burning night and day;
I think I'll just go out and take a rest
For I'm too tired to do my best;

Besides I am so very small
I doubt if I'd be missed at all."
Then a child lovingly touched the light,
"Look, mother, this one shines so very bright.

I think of all the lights upon the tree
This one looks the best to me."
"Oh my goodness," said the light
"I almost dimmed right out of sight.

I thought perhaps no one would care
If I failed to shine my share."
With that a glorious brilliance came
For every light had felt the same.

Our gospel, like this Christmas tree,
With little lights, which are you and me,
We each have a space that we must fill
With love, and lessons and goodwill.

Let's keep our tree ablaze with light,
With testimonies burning bright.
For our gospel is a living tree
That lights the way to eternity.

The holly and the ivy,
When they are both full grown,
Of all the trees that are in the wood,
The holly bears the crown.

O the rising of the sun,
And the running of the deer,
The playing of the merry organ,
Sweet singing in the choir.

E is for Emmanuel

All of this happened to fulfill the Lord's message through his prophet: "Look! The virgin will conceive a child! She will give birth to a son, and he will be called Immanuel (meaning, God is with us)." (Matthew 1:22–23)

The birth of Jesus shows once and for all that God is not above us or against us but rather AMONG us. With the birth of Jesus Christ, God has truly become "Emmanuel", God with us. Therefore the birth of Jesus is the most extraordinary and important event in history. At a moment in time, the infinite became an infant. Almighty God became a human being in a manger.

Common folks can't visit the palaces of newborn kings uninvited (and we seldom are). But kings and princes can visit mangers, and so can bakers and weavers, wise men and shopkeepers, priests and children, cattle and sheep.

This reality is so simple that it is easy to miss. The God-child was announcing in a dramatic way that he had come to be available, to be accessible. He hadn't come to isolate himself, or to hobnob with only the important people. He had come to mingle with all, to receive them with open arms and put himself at their disposal. All this he conveyed by simply being found *lying in a manger.*

Dan Schaeffer

A Sunday-School teacher of pre-schoolers was concerned that her students might be a little confused about Jesus Christ because of the Christmas season emphasis on his birth. He wanted to make sure they understood that the birth of Jesus occurred for real. He asked his class, "Where is Jesus today?"

Steven raised his hand and said, "He's in heaven."

Mary was called on and answered, "He's in my heart." Little Johnny, waving his hand furiously, blurted out, "I know, I know! He's in our bathroom!!!"

The whole class got very quiet, looked at the teacher, and waited for a response. The teacher was completely at a loss for a few very long seconds. Finally, he gathered his wits and asked Little Johnny how he knew this. Little Johnny said,

"Well … every morning, my father gets up, bangs on the bathroom door, and yells, "Good Lord, are you still in there?!"

It was the US astronaut Hale Irwin who said, after he had returned to earth after standing on the moon: "The most significant achievement of our age is not that man stood on the moon, but rather that God in Christ stood upon this earth."

From his deathbed, John Wesley said, "The greatest of all, is, God with us." The present of Christmas is God's presence. "They shall call his name Emmanuel, which translated means, 'God with us'" (Matthew 1:23).

The mystery of the humanity of Christ, that he sank himself into our flesh, is beyond all human understanding.
Martin Luther, *Table Talk*

A grandfather went into a bedroom to find his baby grandson jumping up and down in a playpen, crying his eyes out. When he saw his grandfather, he reached out his little hands and cried, "Out Grandpa, out!" But Grandpa knew that the little boy had been put there as a punishment for bad behaviour. So he said, "No, son, in, in …" But the little child kept crying. His plaintive tears and his outstretched hands reached deep into his heart. What was he to do? The boy must have the punishment, but the grandfather was desperate to comfort him.

Finally, love found a way. Grandpa couldn't take the boy out of the playpen, so he climbed in with him …

Lying at your feet is your dog. Imagine, for the moment, that your dog and every dog is in deep distress. Some of us love dogs very much. If it would help all the dogs in the world to become like men, would you be willing to become a dog? Would you put down your human nature, leave your loved ones, your job, hobbies, your art and literature and music, and choose instead of the intimate communion with your beloved, the poor substitute of looking into the beloved's face and wagging your tail, unable to smile or speak? Christ by becoming man limited the thing which to him was the most precious thing in the world; his unhampered, unhindered communion with the Father.

C S Lewis

History is littered with examples of men who would become gods, but only one example of God becoming man.

How could anyone be afraid of a God who became a child! A God who became so small could only be love and mercy.
St Thérèse of Lisieux

Like your landlord becoming your lodger
Like your managing director up before you for an interview
Like Beethoven queuing up for a ticket to his own concert
Like a headmaster getting the cane
Like a good architect living in a slum built by a rival
Like Picasso painting by numbers –
God lived among us.

Steve Turner

The Christmas story is precisely the story of one grand miracle, the Christian assertion being that what is beyond all space and time, what is uncreated, eternal, came into nature, into human nature, descended into his own universe, and rose again, bringing nature up with him. It is precisely one great miracle. If you take that away there is nothing specifically Christian left. There may be many admirable human things which Christianity shares with all other systems in the world, but there would be nothing specifically Christian.

C S Lewis

Great as he was, Caesar Augustus is now only an echo of ancient times, while the name of the Child he had never heard of is spoken by millions with reverence and love.

Walter Russell Bowie

In our darkest hours, in our saddest moments, when fear and violence and loneliness seem to rule the planet, let us take comfort that we are not alone. Emmanuel. God is with us.

Rose Gallion

There was a Scottish farmer who did not believe in the Christmas story. The idea that God would become a man was absurd. His wife, however, was a devout believer and raised their children in her faith. The farmer sometimes gave her a hard time, mocking her faith and belief in the incarnation of God in the baby of Bethlehem. "It's all nonsense," he said. "Why would God lower himself to become a human like us? It's such a ridiculous story."

One snowy Sunday evening his wife took the children to church while the farmer relaxed at home. After they had left, the weather deteriorated into a blinding snowstorm. Then he heard a loud thump against the window. Then another thump! He ventured outside to see what was happening. There in the field was the strangest sight, a flock of geese! They had been migrating south but had become disorientated by the storm. They were stranded on his farm, unable to fly or to see their way.

The farmer had compassion on them. He wanted to help them and realised his barn would give them shelter for the night. He opened the barn doors and stood back, hoping they would make their way in. But they didn't realise it would be shelter for them. So he tried to shoo the geese in, but they ran in all directions. Perplexed, he got some bread and made a trail to the barn door. But they still didn't catch on. Nothing he could do would get them into the warmth and shelter of the barn.

Feeling totally frustrated, he exclaimed, "Why don't they follow me? Can't they see this is the only place where they can survive the storm? How can I possibly get them to follow me?" He thought for a moment and then realised that they would not follow a human. He said to himself, "How can I possibly save them? The only way would be for me to become a goose. If only I could become like one of them. Then I could save them. They would follow me and I would lead them to safety."

At that moment he stopped and realised what he had said. The words reverberated in his head. "If only I could become like one of them, then I could save them." Then, at last he understood God's heart towards mankind. He fell on his knees in the snow and worshipped him!

We are no longer alone; God is with us. We are no longer homeless; a bit of the eternal home itself has moved into us. Therefore we adults can rejoice deeply within our hearts under the Christmas tree, perhaps more than the children are able. We know that God's goodness will once again draw near.

Dietrich Bonhoeffer

Jill Briscoe once had to speak at a church in Croatia where 200 newly arrived refugees were gathered. Her audience was mostly women because the men were either dead or imprisoned or at war. After seeing the women's faces she felt that her message was totally inappropriate for them. So she prayed for God to give her the words to say. Putting aside her notes she started to tell the women about Jesus and how as a child he had become a refugee himself. She told of how his parents had had to flee to Egypt pursued by Herod's soldiers and how they had left everything behind. She told of the rest of Jesus' life too, and finished by describing what Jesus had suffered on the cross. She told it as it was, not like in the pictures – Jesus, hanging naked on the cross. She finished her message by saying, "All these things have happened to you. You are homeless. You have had had to flee. You have suffered unjustly. But you didn't have a choice. He had a choice. He knew all this would happen to him but he still came." Then Jill told them why. Many of the refugees knelt down, put their hands in the air, and wept. "He's the only one who really understands," they cried.

Christ, by highest heaven adored:
Christ, the everlasting Lord!
Late in time behold him come,
Offspring of the virgin's womb.
Veiled in flesh the God-head see;
Hail the incarnate Deity;
Pleased as man with man to dwell,
Jesus, our Emmanuel.

F is for Families

Jacob was the father of Joseph, the husband of Mary.
Mary was the mother of Jesus, who is called the Messiah.
(Matthew 1:16)

The Christmas story revolves around the holy family involving Joseph, Mary and Jesus. Matthew chapter 1 provides the genealogy or family tree that lies behind this holy family. What is really interesting is the fact that Matthew doesn't attempt to either cover up or erase the really black sheep in that family line. Everyone is mentioned – the good, the bad, and the plain ugly. What a refreshing sign of reality and integrity this is! Most of us have some pretty unsavoury ancestors and most of us have some black sheep in our families today. Family life at Christmas – with its reunions and parties – can be the perfect occasion for the reappearance of demanding family members and the re-emergence of negative character traits!

I well remember a Christmas carol service when I had just been ordained a priest. A lady called Joan had been asked to read Matthew 1:1–17 and had chosen her own introduction to this passage of Scripture. In a packed church she walked proudly to the microphone and said,

"The reading is from Matthew chapter 1, the Gynaecology of St Matthew."

Many of those who realised what was going on considered it an improvement!

When Christmas bells are swinging
above the fields of snow,
We hear sweet voices ringing from
lands of long ago,
And etched on vacant places
Are half-forgotten faces
Of friends we used to cherish, and
loves we used to know.
Ella Wheeler Wilcox

The Lord Jesus Christ was born of a line of ancestors whom the Evangelist Matthew arranges with artistry into three groups of fourteen patriarchs, fourteen kings and fourteen princes. Among the latter were a number of disreputable characters ... God holds before us this mirror of sinners that we may know that (God) is sent to sinners, and from sinners is willing to be born ...
Martin Luther

There is a rather poignant Christmas story about a little girl who watched her mum and dad getting ready for Christmas. To her, it seemed that dad was preoccupied with burdens and bundles, and mum was concerned about parties and presents, and they just had no time for her. She felt that she was being shoved aside. In fact, it seemed to her that she was always being told, "Would you please get out of the way?"

So one night in December she knelt beside her bed and prayed this prayer: "Our Father, who art in heaven, please forgive us our Christmases as we forgive those who Christmas against us."

Did you know that hanging lights on a Christmas tree is one of the three most stressful situations in an ongoing relationship? The other two danger zones are teaching your mate to drive and wallpapering.

We bring you this list of Things Not To Say When Hanging Lights on the Christmas Tree.

- "You've got two red lights right next to each other, dummy. You're supposed to go yellow, green, red, blue, not yellow, red, red, green, blue ..."
- "Up a little higher. You can reach it. Go on, try."
- "What do you do to these lights when you put them away every year? Tie them in knots?"
- "Give me that!"
- "You've got the whole thing on the tree upside-down. The electric pluggee thing should be down here at the bottom, not up at the top."
- "I don't care if you have found another two strings, I'm done!"
- "You've just wound 'em around and around – I thought we agreed it shouldn't look like a spiral this year."
- "Have you been drinking?"
- "Where's the cat?"

In December 2003 it was reported in the news that German singletons would no longer feel lonely at Christmas. Thanks to a new range of wallpaper featuring life-sized pictures of fake friends, loneliness at Christmas was no longer a problem. Wallpaper depicting photos of fake friends looking at home in every room of the house had become a best-seller in Germany. Designer Susanne Schmidt said, "The friends we provide are not very talkative, but they are guaranteed not to argue with you at Christmas."

Christmas was going to be different this year. The father called a family conference and challenged them to be more disciplined in the management of their time during the busy Christmas season and to curtail excessive spending on gifts. He talked about better relations between visiting relatives and a more congenial atmosphere around their home. He brought his speech to a crescendo with his final rallying cry, "Let's make this the best Christmas EVER!" His little son countered the big motivational speech by noting, "But, Dad, I don't see how we could ever improve on the first Christmas."

Christmas is a time when you get homesick — even when you're home.
Carol Nelson

Happy, happy Christmas, that can win us back to the delusions of our childish days; that can recall to the old man the pleasures of his youth; that can transport the sailor and the traveller, thousands of miles away, back to his own fireside and his quiet home!
Charles Dickens, *The Pickwick Papers*, 1836

Now to the Lord sing praises,
All people in this place!
With Christian love and fellowship
Each other now embrace,
And let this Christmas festival
All bitterness displace:

And it's tidings of comfort and joy
Comfort and joy,
And it's tidings of comfort and joy.

G is for Gifts

You know how full of love and kindness our Lord Jesus Christ was. Though he was very rich, yet for your sakes he became poor, so that by his poverty he could make you rich. (2 Corinthians 8:9)

Christmas time is, for most people, about the giving and receiving of gifts. On Christmas Eve the level of expectancy in the average household rises considerably as the children's excitement at the prospect of receiving presents reaches fever pitch. Getting the kids to sleep in such a state of heightened expectation is of course an annual challenge. But once they are asleep, parents have the fun of filling stockings and hanging them at the ends of the children's beds. The presents, carefully wrapped, already wait underneath the Christmas tree. Then, on Christmas Day, there is the joy of seeing happy faces light up as gifts are unwrapped. All this of course is a wonderful reminder of the greatest gift ever given. The gift our Father in heaven gave to us of his Son Jesus Christ. Through Jesus Christ, God has made us spiritually rich. He achieved this by himself becoming poor and being born as a humble infant in a manger. Our gifts at Christmas mean very little if they do not point to the greatest gift of all – a gift that really does have some eternal value and usefulness! As my friend J John says, "At Christmas time, when we receive presents we don't really need, God offers us a gift we cannot do without."

Christmas is based on an exchange of gifts: the gift of God to man – his Son; and the gift of man to God – when we first give ourselves to God.

Vince Havner

Christmas is the season when you buy this year's gifts with next year's money.

The greatest good of every giving is – when the giver is in the gift.

George MacDonald

During his first year at university, Steve couldn't get home for Christmas, so he sent his father a set of inexpensive cufflinks and a note reading, "Dear Dad: This isn't much, but it's all you could afford."

George: My dad's very rich, so I don't know what to get him for Christmas. What do you give to a man who has everything?

Harry: A burglar alarm.

Christmas is a time when we want our past forgotten and our PRESENT remembered.

J John

Christ was content with a stable when he was born so that we could have a mansion when we die.

You can never truly enjoy Christmas until you can look up into the Father's face and tell him you have received HIS Christmas gift, Jesus Christ.
John Rice

It is not the gift, but the thought that counts.

Van Dyke

It was Christmas, and the judge was in a merry mood as he asked the prisoner, "What are you charged with?"

"Doing my Christmas shopping early," replied the defendant.

"That's no offence," said the judge. "How early were you doing this shopping?"

"Before the store opened," countered the prisoner.

Darth Vader and Luke Skywalker were having one of their little father-and-son chats, light sabres drawn and sparks flying.

Vader pinned Luke against a bulkhead and glared into his face. "I know what you're getting for Christmas, Luke," he said. "Oh, yes! I know!"

Luke fought himself free and jumped to a higher platform just out of Vader's reach. "How do you know?" Luke yelled at him. "How do you know what I'm getting for Christmas?"

Darth Vader shot Luke an icy glare, "I felt your presents."

A kindly 90-year-old grandmother found buying presents for family and friends a bit much one Christmas, so she wrote out cheques for all of them, to put in their Christmas cards. In each card she wrote, "Buy your own present", and then sent them off. After the Christmas festivities were over, she found the cheques in her desk! Everyone had got a Christmas card from her with "Buy your own present" written inside, but without the cheques!

A woman was doing her last-minute Christmas shopping and she noticed several boxes of Christmas cards that were marked "reduced". So she thought, "This is great!" and bought a box with 50 cards. She was so happy that she could save money on her Christmas spending.

She went home without looking at the cards or reading the inscription inside. On arriving home, she quickly addressed the envelopes and hastily signed her name in all the cards but one. She rushed them to the post office, mailing all 49 Christmas cards.

Later that night she thought to herself, "I posted all those cards and did not take the time even to sign them."

Imagine her surprise when she picked up the one remaining card to look inside and found the words, "This card is to let you know that a gift is on its way!"

In 1994, two Americans answered an invitation from the Russian Department of Education to teach morals and ethics based on Christian principles. One place they went to was a large orphanage. About 100 boys and girls who had been abandoned, abused, and left in the care of a government-run programme were there. They relate the following story in their own words:

"It was nearing the holiday season, 1994; time for our orphans to hear, for the first time, the traditional story of Christmas. We told them about Mary and Joseph arriving in Bethlehem. Finding no room in the inn, the couple went to a stable, where the baby Jesus was born and placed in a manger.

Throughout the story, the children sat in amazement as they listened. Some sat on the edges of their stools, trying to grasp every word. Completing the story, we gave the children three small pieces of cardboard to make a crude manger. Each child was given a small paper square, cut from yellow napkins I had brought with me. No coloured paper was available in the city. Following instructions, the children tore the paper and carefully laid strips in the manger for straw. Small squares of flannel, cut from a worn-out nightgown an American lady was throwing away as she left Russia, were used for the baby's blanket. A doll-like baby was also created.

All went well until I got to one table, where little Misha sat. He looked to be about six years old and had finished his project. As I looked at the little boy's manger, I was startled to see not one but two babies in the manger. Quickly, I called for the translator to ask the lad why there were two babies in the manger. Crossing his arms in front of him and looking at this completed manger scene, the child began to repeat the story very seriously. For such a young boy, who had only heard the Christmas story once, he related the happenings accurately – until he came to the part where Mary put the baby Jesus in the manger.

Then Misha started to ad-lib. He made up his own ending to the story as he said,

"And when Maria laid the baby in the manger, Jesus looked at me and asked me if I had a place to stay. I told him I have no mamma and I have no papa, so I don't have any place to stay. Then Jesus told me I could stay with him. But I told him I couldn't, because I didn't have a gift to give him like everybody else did. But I wanted to stay with Jesus so much, so I thought about what I had that maybe I could use for a gift. I thought maybe if I kept him warm, that would be a good gift. So I asked Jesus, 'If I keep you warm, will that be a good enough gift?' And Jesus told me, 'If you keep me warm, that will be the best gift anybody ever gave me.' So I got into the manger, and then Jesus looked at me and he told me I could stay with him – for always."

As little Misha finished his story, his eyes brimmed full of tears that splashed down his little cheeks. The little orphan had found someone who would never abandon or abuse him, someone who would stay with him for ever.

A stingy man went Christmas shopping, but everything he saw was too expensive except for a £50 vase that was on sale for £2, because the handle had been broken off. He bought it and had the sales assistant post it so that his friend would think that he had paid £50 for it, and that it had been broken in the mail. A week after Christmas he received a thank-you note from his friend.

"Thank you for the lovely vase," his letter said. "It was so nice of you to wrap each piece separately."

A middle-aged woman posted her Christmas wish list on the refrigerator for her husband to read. Rather than list certain items of desire, she simply requested "something that will make me look sexy and beautiful". When Christmas rolled around she expected to open a package with some fancy lingerie inside. To her surprise, he gave her an exercise bike instead.

Some gifts you can give this Christmas are beyond monetary value: mend a quarrel; dismiss suspicion; tell someone, "I love you". Give something away – anonymously. Forgive someone who has treated you wrong. Turn away wrath with a soft answer. Visit someone in a nursing home. Apologise if you were wrong. Be especially kind to someone with whom you work. Give as God gave to you in Christ, without obligation, or announcement, or reservation, or hypocrisy.

Charles Swindoll

Six-year-old Beth Marsh was asked what she was going to give her brother for Christmas. "I don't know," she answered.

"What did you give him last year?"

"The chicken pox."

The phrases that best sum up the Christmas season? "Peace on earth," "Goodwill to all," and "Batteries not included."

Christmas gift suggestions from Oren Arnold:

- To your enemy, forgiveness
- To an opponent, tolerance
- To a friend, your heart
- To a customer, service
- To all, charity
- To every child, a good example
- To yourself, respect.

In Washington, a TV reporter was working on an assignment called "The Spirit of Christmas", so he called the British Embassy and asked to speak to the British Ambassador.

"Ambassador," the reporter said, "you have been very kind to us through the year and we would like to include you in a Christmas news segment we're going to run. Tell me, what would you like for Christmas?"

The Ambassador replied, "I am very touched by your offer, but I must decline to accept any gift."

"Oh please," said the reporter, "you really have been very helpful to us, so won't you please tell me what you would especially like for Christmas?"

Again the Ambassador refused, but the reporter persisted, and he finally gave in. "All right then, if you insist. This Christmas I would like a jar of mint jelly."

Having forgotten about the conversation, the Ambassador was surprised when, several weeks later, he turned on the evening news and heard the same reporter introducing a segment on "The Spirit of Christmas".

We recently interviewed three visiting ambassadors and asked them what they would like for Christmas. These three diplomats each gave revealing answers when they pondered what they would most like during this Christmas season of goodwill.

The German Ambassador said: "I would like to see a peaceful and prosperous year ahead for all citizens of the planet. May God bless us all."

The Swiss Ambassador said: "May the Spirit of Christmas last throughout the year. It is my dream that our world leaders will be guided toward a common goal of peaceful coexistence. This is my wish this Christmas season."

And then we asked the British Ambassador, who said, "I would like a jar of mint jelly."

Well at least I got what I asked for...

Whatever we try to give to God, no matter how great, will always be less than what he gives us. The Magi travelled far to see him. Yet Jesus had travelled from heaven to find them.

Dan Schaeffer

One Christmas, Santa Claus brought me a toy engine. I took it with me to the convent and played with it while my mother and the nuns discussed old times. A young nun brought us in to see the crib. When I saw the Holy Child in the manger I was distressed, because, little as I had, he had nothing at all. For me it was fresh proof of the incompetence of Santa Claus. I asked the young nun politely if the Holy Child didn't like toys, and she replied composedly enough, "Oh, he does, but his mother was too poor to afford them." That settled it. My mother was too poor too, but at Christmas she at least managed to buy me something even if it was only a box of crayons. I distinctly remember getting into the crib and putting the engine between his outstretched arms. I probably showed him how to wind it as well, because a small baby like that would not be clever enough to know. I remember too the tearful feeling of reckless generosity with which I left him there in the nightly darkness of the chapel, clutching my toy engine to his chest.

Frank O'Connor

A family had twin boys, whose only resemblance to each other was their looks. If one felt it was too hot, the other thought it was too cold. If one said the TV was too loud, the other claimed the volume needed to be turned up. Opposite in every way, one was an eternal optimist, the other a doom-and-gloom pessimist.

Just to see what would happen, at Christmas time their father loaded the pessimist's room with every imaginable toy and game. The optimist's room he loaded with horse manure.

On Christmas Day the father passed by the pessimist's room and found him sitting amid his new gifts crying bitterly.

"Why are you crying?" the father asked.

"Because my friends will be jealous, I'll have to read all these instructions before I can do anything with this stuff, I'll constantly need batteries, and my toys will eventually get broken," answered the pessimist twin.

Passing the optimist twin's room, the father found him dancing for joy in the pile of manure. "What are you so happy about?" he asked.

To which the optimist twin replied, "There's got to be a pony in here somewhere!"

What can I give him,
   Poor as I am?
If I were a shepherd
   I would bring a lamb;
If I were a wise man
   I would do my part;
Yet what I can I give him –
   Give my heart.

Christina Rossetti

H is for Herod

Herod was furious when he learned that the wise men had outwitted him. He sent soldiers to kill all the boys in and around Bethlehem who were two years old and under, because the wise men had told him the star first appeared to them about two years earlier. (Matthew 2:16)

Herod represents all political attempts to destroy Christmas as a festival and to eradicate talk of Jesus from the public domain.

Not long ago an atheistic organisation put up a sign in Madison County, Wisconsin, USA. It was Christmas and they were trying to signal their objections to the season. So they wrote the following words on it:

"In this season of the winter solstice, may reason prevail. There are no gods, no devils, no angels, no heaven, no hell. There is only our material world. Religion is but a myth and superstition that hardens hearts and enslaves minds."

Then, in a strange concession to the very thing they were dismissing, they wrote a warning to thieves on the other side, saying: "Thou Shalt Not Steal".

Herod was the first man who hated Christmas. He was the original Grinch!

Mark Stibbe

The Grinch hated Christmas!
The whole Christmas season!
Now, please don't ask why.
No one quite knows the reason.
It could be that his head wasn't screwed on quite right.
It could be, perhaps, that his shoes were too tight.
But I think that the most likely reason of all
May have been that his heart was two sizes too small.

Dr Seuss

December 2003: the Liberty Counsel USA reports that Michigan schools have recently reversed their practice of segregating religious holiday books, including Hanukkah and Christmas, to prevent students from accessing them. Liberty Counsel President Mathew Staver said his organisation has launched a nationwide campaign to prevent blatant religious discrimination during the holidays.

"We are resolved to stop the Grinch from stealing Christmas," he said.

To avoid offending anybody, an American school dropped religion altogether and started singing about the weather.

At one school, they now hold the winter programme in February and sing unmemorable songs such as "Winter Wonderland", "Frosty the Snowman" and "Suzy Snowflake", all of which is odd because the school in question is in Miami.

The pastor of a church put up a sign in front of his church during the Advent season, which said, "Jesus is the reason for the season. Merry Christmas". He received a complaint from a woman in the community who took exception to the message. She closed the conversation by saying, "I don't think the church should try to drag religion into every holiday."

The Supreme Court has ruled that they cannot have a nativity scene in Washington, DC. This wasn't for any religious reasons. They couldn't find three wise men and a virgin.

Jay Leno

Even Christians can be like Herod in relation to stamping out Christmas. Many years ago the Puritans objected to the fact that Christmas Day usually happened on a weekday, therefore distracting people, they thought, from the proper observance of Sunday worship. They disposed of Christmas altogether. In Puritan settlements across 17th-century America a law was passed outlawing the celebration of Christmas. The marketplace was ordered to stay open for business and all violators were prosecuted. It was against the law to make plum pudding on December 25th and the day was not referred to as Yuletide but as fool-tide.

Herod is missing from the manger scene.
Dan Schaeffer

Listen to modern day Puritan Upton Sinclair: "Consider Christmas – could Satan in his most malignant mood have devised a worse combination of graft plus bunkum than the system whereby several hundred million people get a billion or so gifts for which they have no use, and some thousands of shop clerks die of exhaustion while selling them and every other child in the Western world is made ill by overeating – all in the name of the lowly Jesus."

Bill Jamieson wrote an article in *The Scotsman* in December 2003 on the topic, "The State is trying to kill off Christmas". He wrote:

People have long bemoaned the commercialisation of Christmas. But there is another, graver, threat to the spirit of this religious festival: "a growing assertion by the state that Christmas would be better celebrated without Christianity at all". This year, the Scottish Parliament banned its officials from sending Christmas cards with a religious theme. Church officials in High Wycombe, meanwhile, were prevented from advertising a carol service in local libraries for fear it would offend non-Christians. Such are the sacrifices demanded by the high priests of social inclusion. The card that best captures the new manners is the one sent by the Culture Secretary Tessa Jowell. It is a postmodern collage featuring ethnic tribal dancers, a television set, a train and the word "goal". Short of sending out an entirely blank card, Ms Jowell has absolutely got it: none of the images is Christian, or even seasonal. This is how the modern state would have us celebrate Christ's birth: with meaningless prattle as proxy for faith.

December 2003

Whereas the wise men were prepared to travel a thousand miles to worship the child born as "King of the Jews", Herod could not be bothered to travel five miles to pay him a visit.

If we leave Herod in the Christmas narrative, we can address the shadow of evil hovering over Christmas to this day. Herod still stalks the earth. He may be disguised in the military fatigues of a dictator. He murders street children in Brazil by sending death squads when darkness falls. Herod sells Thai children as prostitutes to wealthy westerners. He detonates a car bomb that kills innocent people.

Kerry Bond

Herod, then, with fear was filled:
"A prince," he said, "in Jewry!"
All the little boys he killed
At Beth-lem in his fury,
At Beth-lem in his fury.

I is for Innkeeper

And while they were there, the time came for her baby to be born. She gave birth to her first child, a son. She wrapped him snugly in strips of cloth and laid him in a manger, because there was no room for them in the village inn. (Luke 2:6–7)

The innkeeper is one of the favourite characters in the nativity story. Yet no innkeeper is mentioned in Luke's account, or in Matthew's, for that matter. As the passage above clearly shows, no character of this description is mentioned. They are inferred from the text. Nevertheless, there is little doubt that the innkeeper must have played at least some part in the actual events; if nothing else, at least to say "put them round the back in the place where the animals are". The innkeeper's role has therefore become an opportunity for a lot of important lessons about offering hospitality.

During the winter of 1926, Thelma Goldstein treated herself to her first real vacation in Florida.

Being unfamiliar with the area, she wandered into a restricted hotel in North Miami. "Excuse me," she said to the manager. "My name is Mrs Goldstein, and I'd like a small room for two weeks."

"I'm awfully sorry," he replied, "but all of our rooms are occupied."

Just as he said that, a man came down and checked out. "What luck," said Mrs Goldstein. "Now there's a room."

"Not so fast, madam. I'm sorry, but this hotel is restricted. No Jews allowed."

"Jewish? Who's Jewish? I happen to be Catholic."

"I find that hard to believe. Let me ask you, who was the Son of God?"

"Jesus, Son of Mary."

"Where was he born?"

"In a stable."

"And why was he born in a stable?"

"Because a schmuck like you wouldn't let a Jew rent a room in his hotel!"

> *Christianity should be characterised by the open hand, the open heart and the open door.*
> William Barclay

There was a little old cleaning woman who went to the local church. When the invitation was given at the end of the service, she went forward, wanting to become a member. The pastor listened as she told him how she had accepted Jesus and wanted to be baptised and become a member of the church. The pastor thought to himself, "Oh my, she is so unkempt, even smells a little, and her fingernails are not clean. She picks up garbage, cleans toilets – what would the members think of her?" He told her that she needed to go home and pray about it and then decide.

The following week, there she was again. She told the pastor that she had prayed about it and still wanted to be baptised.

"I have passed this church for so long. It is so beautiful, and I truly want to become a member."

Again the pastor told her to go home and pray some more.

A few weeks later, while out eating at a restaurant, the pastor saw the little old lady. He did not want her to think that he was ignoring her, so he approached her and said, "I have not seen you for a while. Is everything all right?"

"Oh, yes," she said. "I talked with Jesus, and he told me not to worry about becoming a member of your church."

"He did?" said the pastor.

"Oh, yes," she replied. "He said even he hasn't been able to get into your church yet, and he's been trying for years."

Christmas is the season for kindling the fire of hospitality in the hall, the genial flame of charity in the heart.

Washington Irving

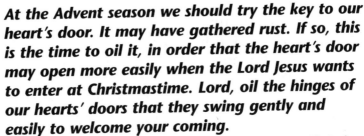

At the Advent season we should try the key to our heart's door. It may have gathered rust. If so, this is the time to oil it, in order that the heart's door may open more easily when the Lord Jesus wants to enter at Christmastime. Lord, oil the hinges of our hearts' doors that they swing gently and easily to welcome your coming.

Prayer of a New Guinea Christian

A little boy was really disappointed about not being chosen to play Joseph in the school nativity play. He was given the role of the innkeeper instead, and over the weeks leading up to the play he plotted his revenge. The day of the performance came. Mary and Joseph came to the inn and knocked on the door. The innkeeper opened the door a crack and looked at them coldly.

"Can you give us a room for the night?" asked Joseph.

Then the innkeeper flung the door open wide, beamed at them and said, "Come in, come in! You can have the best room in the hotel!"

There was a pause. But Joseph was a quick thinker. He looked over the innkeeper's shoulder, then turned to Mary and said,

"We're not staying in a dump like that. Come on, Mary, we'll sleep in the stable!"

Well-to-do families in Serbia keep open house for three days at Christmas, and all visitors – friends or enemies, strangers or beggars – are welcome to come to the table. On Christmas Eve, the Serbians have a saying: "Tonight earth is blended with Paradise."

If we open our hearts and embrace him … not only to reap abundance and joy and health and happy fulfilment, but also the cancellation of sins – then this is the greatest welcome we can give to the Christ child.
Norman Vincent Peale

News Item, December 2004

A British hotel chain is offering couples called Mary and Joseph a free night's stay over Christmas.

"We are trying to make up for the hotel industry not having any rooms left on Christmas Eve 2004 years ago," said Sandy Leckie, manager of the Travelodge hotel in London's Covent Garden.

"Our hotel is definitely more comfortable than a stable. I just hope they don't bring their donkey," he said. But the offer has just one proviso – the couples have to produce identification showing their names.

Joy to the world! The Lord is come:
Let earth receive her King.
Let ev'ry heart prepare Him room,
And heaven and nature sing,
And heaven and nature sing,
And heaven and heaven and
nature sing.

J is for Joseph

When Joseph woke up, he did what the angel of the Lord commanded. He brought Mary home to be his wife, but she remained a virgin until her son was born. And Joseph named him Jesus. (Matthew 1:24–25)

Joseph is definitely the forgotten hero of the nativity story. According to Jewish law at the time, at the very least he was entitled to break off the betrothal process and technically divorce his bride. But he was given a dream, and in that dream told what he must do. Even though the child to be born was not his own, Joseph stood faithfully by Mary and was a father to Jesus as the boy grew up. In our own time, when fatherlessness has become an epidemic, Joseph's example is a powerful one. Though some still ignore or undermine his part in the nativity, others are beginning to highlight Joseph as a very modern example.

David Beckham glories in it. So does the new Archbishop of Canterbury. Now, at long last, it's time for Joseph to celebrate fatherhood too.

Jack O'Sullivan, 2002

One of my favourite Christmas stories is about the infant-school nativity play where one little boy was desperate to play the part of Joseph.

The day came when the teacher announced the parts and the little boy was NOT chosen to play Joseph. However, he WAS asked to play the role of the innkeeper.

Even though he had been picked, he was still not happy. The day arrived for the performance of the play. The entire school was there. There were parents, grandparents, teachers and governors in the audience.

Mary and Joseph arrived at the inn and Joseph knocked on the door.

"Can my wife and I come in?" There was a pause, and then the little boy replied, "SHE can come in but YOU can't." He then said, "I wanted to be Joseph!"

Several Christmases ago, a major chain of UK stores had nativity sets or Christmas cribs in all their shops. But in each one the figure of Joseph was missing. In an extraordinary show of political correctness, the partnership issued a statement saying, "We have to provide for all our customers the nativity scene that they need".

Scientific research is now being carried out that could one day allow babies to be conceived without fathers. Doctors in Australia have demonstrated how eggs can be fertilised with cells from any part of the body – not just sperm. The experiments with mice are at a very early stage. But already they have prompted speculation that lesbian couples could in future have daughters that are genetically their own. If the technique worked in humans, men would no longer need to be involved in the business of reproduction.

The Australian researchers, led by Dr Orly Lacham-Kaplan from Monash University, Melbourne, are investigating spermless fertilisation to help men who cannot father babies. They have succeeded in "fertilising" a normal mouse egg using a cell taken from the body of a male. The Society for the Protection of the Unborn Child (SPUC) reacted with outrage. "Suggesting that we can do without fathers is part of an increasing attempt to disassociate childbearing from the concept that it's something given to us which is natural."

Daughter: *"Is it true that Santa Claus brings us our Christmas presents?"*

Mother: *"Yes, that's true."*

Daughter: *"And the stork brings us babies?"*

Mother: *"Yes, that's true."*

Daughter: *"And the Police Department protects us?"*

Mother: *"That's right."*

Daughter: *"Then what do we need Daddy for?"*

A mother and daughter are shopping at Christmas time, when the mother eyes an expensive fur coat. "This year," she says, "I think that I will buy my present instead of making you and Dad shop for me."

The daughter nods in agreement.

"And I think this fur coat would be perfect too."

The daughter protests, "But, Mum, some helpless, poor creature has to suffer so that you can have this."

"Don't worry, sweetheart," says the mother, "your father won't get the bill until after Christmas."

A Sunday-school teacher asked her class, "What was Jesus' mother's name?"

One child answered, "Mary."

The teacher then asked, "Who knows what Jesus' father's name was?"

A little kid said, "Verge."

Confused, the teacher asked, "Where did you get that from?"

The kid said, "Well, you know how they are always talking about 'Verge and Mary'."

"Joseph dearest, Joseph mine,
Help me cradle the child divine;
God reward thee and All that's thine
In paradise,"
So prays the mother Mary.

K is for Kings

Jesus was born in the town of Bethlehem in Judea, during the reign of King Herod. About that time some wise men from eastern lands arrived in Jerusalem, asking, "Where is the newborn king of the Jews?" (Matthew 2:1–2)

It's like a game show. We could call it, "Will the real king please stand up?". The story starts with King Herod, a puppet ruler whose strings were pulled by the Romans. Then there were the wise men, the magi, wrongly called "kings" in the carol "We three kings" (and there probably weren't three of them either!). Then there is the baby in the manger, whom the wise men call "the newborn king of the Jews". Which of these was the real king? The answer of course is a surprise. The most powerful ruler in the whole sequence of events is the tiny, vulnerable infant in an animal's feeding trough.

Three kings came to see the king and asked him where the new king was born. But the first king told the three kings that he didn't know where the second king was. His advisers looked in the Bible – though not in First or Second Kings – and found that the second king was to be born in Bethlehem. So the first king told the three kings to find the second king and tell him, the first king, where the second king was, because the first king thought the second king was one king too many. But when the three kings found the second king they realised he was actually the number-one king – the King of Kings – and that, compared with him, the other king and all other kings were really no kings at all.

The TOP SEVEN things overheard on the Wise Men's Journey to Bethlehem:

7. Man, I'm starting to get a rush from this frankincense!
6. You guys ever eat camel meat? I hear it tastes like goat.
5. You know, I used to go to school with a girl name Beth Lehem.
4. What kind of name is Balthazar anyhow? Phoenician?
3. Hey, do either of you know why "MYRRH" is spelled with a "Y" instead of a "U"?
2. Okay, whose camel just spat?

And the NUMBER ONE thing overheard on the Wise Men's journey to Bethlehem …

1. All this staring at a star while riding a camel is making me woozy.

What if the three wise men had been three wise women?

Well, they would have asked for directions and arrived on time, helped deliver the baby, cleaned the stable, brought a casserole and given the child much more practical gifts.

Three young children were playing the parts of the wise men in a school nativity play. At one point they came to Mary and Joseph at the manger and said the following:

Magi 1: *Here, this is gold.*
Magi 2: *This is myrrh.*
Magi 3: *And Frank sent this.*

The scene of proud and richly-costumed sages worshipping a baby in the humblest of circumstances has etched itself on the world's imagination, for it is a graphic study in contrasts. The gifts they presented are usually interpreted symbolically. Gold, a royal gift, signified Jesus' kingship. Frankincense, a fragrant gum resin burned as incense, denoted his future priesthood. The third gift, myrrh, called smyrna in Greek, was an aromatic orange-coloured resin from the small, thorny trees of the Cammiphora family. Myrrh was expensive and much esteemed for use in perfumes, anointing oil, medicine and embalming. That, years later, the crucified Jesus was offered wine mixed with myrrh as a palliative (Mark 15:23) and was also buried with the substance (John 19:39) renders this gift predictive enough.

Paul Maier

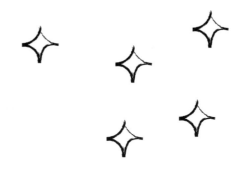

The simple shepherds heard the voice of an angel and found their Lamb; the wise men saw the light of a star and found their Wisdom.
Fulton John Sheen

Wise men still seek him ...

We are accustomed to thinking that the greatest gift of the Magi was gold, frankincense and myrrh. It wasn't. The greatest gift they brought was their devotion; their willingness to endure whatever it took and to look as long as it took to find what God had promised them through the sign. Their physical gifts paled in comparison.
Dan Schaeffer

Who are the wise men now, when all is told?
Not men of science; nor the great and strong;
Not those whose eager hands pile high the gold;
But those amid the tumult and the throng
Who follow still the Star of Bethlehem.

B Y Williams

Popular talk-show host Larry **King** was once asked the question, "If you could select any one person across all of history to interview, who would it be?" Larry King answered that he would like to interview Jesus Christ. When the questioner asked what he would ask Jesus, King replied: "I would like to ask him if he was indeed virgin-born. The answer to that question would define history for me."

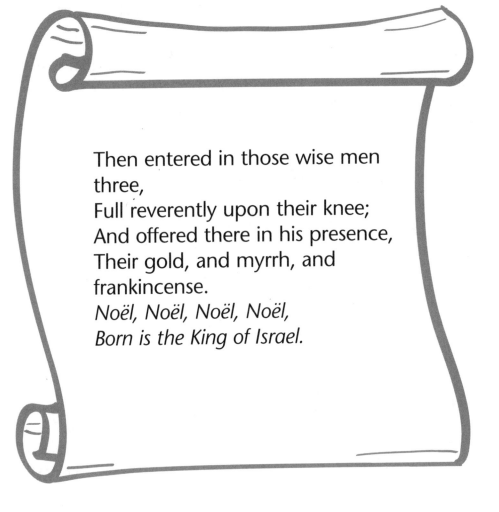

Then entered in those wise men three,
Full reverently upon their knee;
And offered there in his presence,
Their gold, and myrrh, and frankincense.
Noël, Noël, Noël, Noël,
Born is the King of Israel.

L is for Love

For God so loved the world that he gave his only Son, so that everyone who believes in him will not perish but have eternal life. God did not send his Son into the world to condemn it, but to save it.
(John 3:16–17)

Christmas is the ultimate love story. God let his one and only Son leave the comfort and glory of heaven to come to earth to be crucified for our sins. God in effect gave away what was most precious to himself, his own dear Son. As for the Son, he was prepared to humble himself and be born as a baby. At the end of his life he allowed himself to experience the most excruciating execution human beings have ever devised. Why? All because of great, self-sacrificial love. Christmas is truly the greatest love story of all time. It is a season in which we are reminded of the importance of loving others, of giving rather than receiving.

Probably the reason we all go so haywire
at Christmastime with the endless
unrestrained and often silly buying of gifts
is that we don't quite know how to put
our love into words.

Harlan Miller

Unless we make Christmas an
occasion to share our
blessings, all the snow in
Alaska won't make it "white".
Bing Crosby

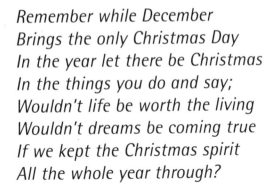

Remember while December
Brings the only Christmas Day
In the year let there be Christmas
In the things you do and say;
Wouldn't life be worth the living
Wouldn't dreams be coming true
If we kept the Christmas spirit
All the whole year through?

At a monastery high in the mountains, the monks have a rigid vow of silence. Only at Christmas, and only by one monk, and only with one sentence, is the vow allowed to be broken. One Christmas, Brother Thomas is allowed to speak, and he says, "I like the mashed potatoes we have with the Christmas turkey!" and he sits down.

Silence ensues for 365 days. The next Christmas, Brother Michael gets his turn, and he says, "I think the mashed potatoes are lumpy and I hate them!"

Once again, silence for 366 days (it's leap year). The following Christmas, Brother Paul rises and says, "I am fed up with this constant bickering!"

> Christmas, my child, is love in action. Every time we love, every time we give, it's Christmas.
>
> **Dale Evans**

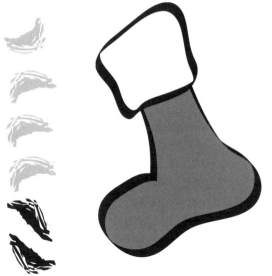

Let us remember that the Christmas heart is a giving heart, a wide-open heart that thinks of others first. The birth of the baby Jesus stands as the most significant event in all history, because it has meant the pouring into a sick world of the healing medicine of love, which has transformed all manner of hearts for almost two thousand years …
Underneath all the bulging bundles is this beating Christmas heart.

George Matthew Adams

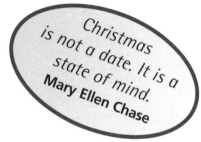

Christmas is not a date. It is a state of mind.
Mary Ellen Chase

Next to a circus, there ain't nothing that packs up and tears out faster than the Christmas spirit.

Kin Hubbard

Blessed is the season which engages the whole world in a conspiracy of love.
Hamilton Wright Mabie

Christmas is most truly Christmas when we celebrate it by giving the light of love to those who need it most.

Ruth Carter Stapleton

The Price Of True Love

The price of giving all the items bestowed by the "true love" of the song "The Twelve Days of Christmas" may be a little beyond most people's budget. The following costs were calculated for 1998, based upon a report issued in 1995 by PNC Bank Corp., assuming an annual rate of inflation of 2.5 per cent:

1. Partridge in a pear tree £20
2. Turtle doves £25
3. French hens £10
4. Calling birds £150
5. Gold rings £250
6. Geese-a-laying £100
7. Swans-a-swimming £4,000
8. Maids-a-milking £20
9. Pipers piping £1,500
10. Ladies dancing £1,500
11. Lords-a-leaping £500
12. Drummers drumming £750

Total to give gifts once = £8,825

Singing the song in its entirety results in 364 presents …

Love came down at Christmas,
Love all lovely, love divine;
Love was born at Christmas;
Star and angels gave the sign.

Worship we the Godhead,
Love incarnate, love divine;
Worship we our Jesus,
But wherewith for sacred sign?

Love shall be our token;
Love shall be yours and love be mine;
Love to God and to all men,
Love for plea and gift and sign.

Christina Rossetti

M is for Mary

Mary responded, "I am the Lord's servant, and I am willing to accept whatever he wants. May everything you have said come true." And then the angel left. (Luke 1:38)

Christmas is a challenging time for mothers. We mustn't forget that it was a very trying time for the mother involved in the original story. Mary had said yes to Joseph's proposal and was waiting for the consummation of her marriage on Joseph's return. Mary was probably only about fifteen years old at the time. As she waited, she was visited by an angel and told that she was going to become pregnant by the Holy Spirit. Even though Mary was probably little more than a teenager, she faced this unprecedented task with simple obedience saying, "I am willing". Mary is therefore a great example to everyone, especially mothers. She is history's most famous mother.

Edna Bowman's parody of the
Twelve Days of Christmas:

"On the twelfth day of Christmas
My littlest love gave to me
Twelve dogs a-leaping
Eleven cats a-creeping
Ten fingers gripping
Nine toes a-tripping
Eight drinks a-spilling
Seven glasses filling
Six friends and things
Five telephone rings
Four crayoned walls
Three loud calls
Two kisses free
And one mother up a pear tree."

After a long day of putting on a wonderful Christmas meal, Mum was standing over the kitchen sink wearily washing the mountain of dirty dishes. In the middle of this monumental task, her teenage daughter strolled into the kitchen and saw what her mother was doing. The thoughtful girl said, "Mum, today's a holiday, you shouldn't be doing that." The mother was taken aback by the seeming kindness of her daughter. She began to put down the dish rag and take off her gloves. A sense of pride overtook her as she thought her little girl was now starting to show signs of maturity by helping out with the dishes. Her bubble was burst, though, when the teenager said, "Just do them tomorrow."

A Mother's Story

My husband and I had been happily (most of the time) married for five years but hadn't been blessed with a baby. I decided to do some serious praying and promised God that if he would give us a child, I would be a perfect mother, love it with all my heart and raise it with his Word as my guide.

God answered my prayers and blessed us with a son. The next year, God blessed us with another son. The following year, he blessed us with yet another son. The year after that, we were blessed with a daughter. My husband thought we'd been blessed right into poverty. We now had four children, and the oldest was only four years old. I learned never to ask God for anything unless I meant it. As a minister once told me, "If you pray for rain, make sure you carry an umbrella."

I began reading a few verses of the Bible to the children each day as they played in their cribs. I was off to a good start. God had entrusted me with four children and I didn't want to disappoint him. I tried to be patient the day the children smashed two dozen eggs on the kitchen floor searching for baby chicks. I tried to be understanding when they started a hotel for homeless frogs in the spare bedroom, although it took me nearly two hours to catch all 23 frogs. When my daughter poured ketchup over herself and rolled up in a blanket to see how it felt to be a hot dog, I tried to see the humour rather than the mess.

In spite of changing over 25,000 nappies, never eating a hot meal and never sleeping for more than 30 minutes at a time, I still thank God daily for my children. While I couldn't keep my promise to be a perfect mother – I didn't even come close – I *did* keep my promise to raise them in the Word of God.

My proudest moment came during the children's Christmas pageant. My daughter was playing Mary, two of my sons were shepherds and my youngest son was a wise man. This was their moment to shine. My five-year-old shepherd had practised his line, "We found the babe wrapped in swaddling clothes". But he was nervous and said, "The baby was wrapped in wrinkled clothes." My four-year-old "Mary" said, "That's not 'wrinkled clothes,' silly. That's dirty, rotten clothes." A wrestling match broke out between Mary and the shepherd and was stopped by an angel, who bent her halo and lost her left wing. I slouched a little lower in my seat when Mary dropped the doll representing Baby Jesus, and it bounced down the aisle crying, "Mamamama". Mary grabbed the doll, wrapped it back up and held it tightly as the wise men arrived. My other son stepped forward wearing a bathrobe and a paper crown, knelt at the manger and announced, "We are the three wise men, and we are bringing gifts of gold, common sense and fur."

The congregation dissolved into laughter, and the pageant got a standing ovation.

"I've never enjoyed a Christmas programme as much as this one," Father Brian laughed, wiping tears from his eyes. "For the rest of my life, I'll never hear the Christmas story without thinking of gold, common sense and fur."

"My children are my pride and my joy and my greatest blessing," I said as I dug through my handbag for an aspirin.

A church produced a Christmas play a few years ago. A young boy had only one line. He was to stand and say, "I am the light of the world". However, on the night of the production, he froze at the sight of so many people and forgot his line. His mother was seated in the front row and began mouthing his line for him. Following her cue, he said, "My Mother is the light of the world."

A child's comment: "When Mary heard that she was to be the mother of Jesus she sang the Magna Carta."

In order that the body of Christ might be shown to be a real body, he was born of a woman. In order that his Godhead might be made clear, he was born of a Virgin.

Thomas Aquinas (1225–1274)

Human history as we have told it has usually been the story of human males, the story of power and accomplishment (often in the name of God) of statesmen, warriors, explorers, entrepreneurs, philosophers and so on. But now in the most important event of all history the mighty male is excluded! It is a woman who is the agent of God's work in the world and gives us the first and prime example of the proper role of human beings in relation to God and God's work. Mary's modest "Let it be done with me according to your word" tells all of us, male and female alike, that our task is to bear witness to God's and not our own greatness, to be the servants and not the sponsors of God in the world.

Shirley C Guthrie

At a nativity play, all was going well until the angel appeared and told the little girl playing Mary that she was going to have a baby.

"But how can this be," said Mary, "since I am a Viking?"

We are the mother of Christ when we carry him in our heart and body by love and a pure and sincere conscience. And we give birth to him through our holy works, which ought to shine on others by our example.

St Francis of Assisi

Little Johnny went to his mother, demanding a new bicycle. His mother decided that he should take a look at himself and the way he acted. She said, "Well, Johnny, it isn't Christmas and we don't have the money to just go out and buy you anything you want. So why don't you write a letter to Jesus and pray for one instead?"

After his temper tantrum his mother sent him to his room. He finally sat down to write a letter to Jesus:

Dear Jesus,
I've been a good boy this year and would appreciate a new bicycle.
Your friend,
Johnny

Now Johnny knew that Jesus really knew what kind of boy he was (a brat), so he ripped up the letter and decided to give it another try.

Dear Jesus,
I've been an OK boy this year and I want a new bicycle.
Yours truly,
Johnny

Well, Johnny knew this wasn't totally honest, so he tore it up and tried again.

Dear Jesus,
I've thought about being a good boy this year and can I have a bicycle?
Johnny

Well, Johnny looked deep down into his heart, which by the way was what his mother really wanted. He knew he had been terrible and was deserving of almost nothing. He crumpled up the letter, threw it in the rubbish bin and went running out of the house. He wandered about aimlessly, depressed because of the way he treated his parents, and really considered his actions. He finally found himself in front of a Catholic church. Johnny went inside and knelt down, looking around, not knowing what he should really do.

Johnny finally got up and began to walk out of the door, looking at all the statues. All of a sudden he grabbed a statue of the Virgin Mary and ran out of the door.

He went home, hid the statue under his bed and wrote this letter:

Jesus,
I've got your mother. If you ever want to see her again, give me a bike.
You know who

Mary, Mary,
What else did the angel tell you?
While you nurtured his message
And pondered the wild potential
Of a womb, did you envision those
Who would come after, the generations
That would Balkanise your heart,
Stamp your image on their banners
And lead you into battle;
That the wind would carry your name
From a German soldier's lips
As he lay dying on the Eastern front,
A Polish captain would wear your medal
Up the heights of Monte Cassino?
Do you grow weary of false sightings
And forced tears, the rote of rosaries,
The bargains of Novenas?
Oh, Lady of Guadalupe,
Madonna of Czestochowa,
Queen of Patriarchs,
Mystical Rose,
Do you sometimes long to cry out
To the complaining Daughters of Eve,
To the rapacious Sons of Adam:
"Stop. Be silent. Listen. Hear me.
I'm Miriam, the Jewish girl from Nazareth
Who said 'yes' to life".

Alice Tarnowski

O that birth forever blessed!
When the Virgin, full of grace,
By the Holy Ghost conceiving,
Bore the Saviour of our race,
And the Babe, the world's Redeemer,
First revealed His sacred face,
Evermore and evermore.

N is for Nativity

An empty stable stays clean, but no income comes from an empty stable. (Proverbs 14:4)

Of course, Christian art has made the nativity scene gloriously hygienic. But the truth is, the stable or cave where Jesus was born would have been smelly, dirty and untidy. Life is like this too. Life is messy rather than neat, orderly and safe. In fact, one teacher who grew up on a farm once said to me, "There is no milk without some manure." In the original nativity scene, there was a lot of trash, I imagine. But the great challenge of Christmas is whether or not we see the treasure in the trash. God often camouflages himself like this. The question is, will we see the miracle in the mess?

The Christmas story reminds us once again it was not man's idea that the Son of God should be born in a stable. And so the first thing we learn from Jesus' birth is that the Lord will not always be found where we expect to find Him. We tend to look for Him in the nice, the clean, the warm. We expect Him to be in churches and in the Bible and in hymns of praise and in Christmas cards which have Scripture verses on them … And if these are the only places we search for the Lord, then we're not looking in the stable.

James F Colaianni

The only person in history who was able to choose where to be born chose a stable.

Christ is revealed only to a few witnesses, and that at dead of night. Further, while God has at hand many of rank and high ability as witnesses, He puts them aside and simply chooses shepherds, of little account with men, of no reckoning … if we desire to come to Christ, we must not be ashamed to follow those whom God chose, from the sheep dung, to bring down the pride of the world.

John Calvin

City officials in
Canada have banned
a donkey from their live animal
nativity scene because it is too violent.

The Christmas stable is set up each December outside
Edmonton City Hall, but this year it will be one ass
short. According to the *Edmonton Sun*
newspaper, the donkey often kicked out
at the three sheep that joined him
alongside the manger.

City spokesman Don Belanger said:
"He had a tendency to be, well, shall
we say, somewhat territorial."

The ark of the covenant in the Old Testament, with its ornate and precious gold inlaid work of beautiful craftsmanship, housed the Shekinah glory of the Lord. Yet a common feeding trough for beasts of burden hosted the God-Child Himself. Whenever I am tempted to blurt out, "Lord, you don't know what it's like to be humiliated like this", He points to the manger. When I cry out, "Lord, I deserve better than this", He points to the manger.

Dan Schaeffer

It happened at Christmas! The leader of the children's department was doing a children's story at Christmas. The presentations were always excellent. This particular year, he had four children to help him tell the story of the star that shone over the stable in Bethlehem the night of the birth of Jesus. At a given signal, each child was to flip over a large piece of cardboard spelling the word, S-T-A-R. Unfortunately, the leader did not realise that the letters would be in the reverse order when the cards were flipped over.

The word that all the people saw was R-A-T-S.

This object lesson was such a surprise that it took some time until the laughter died down and the service could continue.

A perfectly managed Christmas correct in every detail is a sure sign of someone who hasn't enough to do.
Katharine Whitehorn

028

9332 3922

www.ncipher.com

II recently visited the United States, and
hted in spelling out the logistics involved; her
pounds of luggage included two outfits for
urning outfit in case someone died, 40 pints of
id-leather toilet seat covers. She brought along
two valets, and a host of other attendants. A
to a foreign country can easily cost twenty

st, God's visit to earth took place in an animal
ndants present and nowhere to lay the newborn
ugh. Indeed, the event that divided history, and
, into two parts may have had more animal than
A mule could have stepped on him.

Philip Yancey

The Nativity

Among the oxen (like an ox I'm slow)
I see a glory in the stable grow
Which, with the ox's dullness might at length
Give me an ox's strength.

Among the asses (stubborn I as they)
I see my Saviour where I looked for hay;
So may my beastlike folly learn at least
The patience of a beast.

Among the sheep (I like a sheep have strayed)
I watch the manger where my Lord is laid;
Oh that my baa-ing nature would win thence
Some woolly innocence!

C S Lewis

See Him lying on a bed of straw;
A draughty stable with an open door;
Mary cradling the babe she bore;
The Prince of glory is his name.

O is for Origins

Most honourable Theophilus: Many people have written accounts about the events that took place among us. They used as their source material the reports circulating among us from the early disciples and other eyewitnesses of what God has done in fulfilment of his promises. Having carefully investigated all of these accounts from the beginning, I have decided to write a careful summary for you, to reassure you of the truth of all you were taught. (Luke 1:1–4)

Most people's view of what happened at Jesus' birth is based more on fantasy than fact. A great deal of what we remember, sing about and celebrate at Christmas is actually not in the original script, recorded by both Luke and Matthew. It is based on myth and tradition.

W hy is Christmas Day celebrated on December 25th? The winter solstice is the day when there is the shortest time between the sun rising and the sun setting. It happens between December 22nd and December 25th. To the Romans this indicated that the winter was over and spring was on its way. This was the cause of great celebration. The light of the sun had conquered the darkness of winter. The Roman Emperor Aurelian, in the year AD 274, officially declared December 25th as the Birthday of the Unconquered Sun (*dies natalis solis invicti*).

The early church was quick to seize upon the significance of this. Jesus said that he was the light of the world, so the early church regarded this time as appropriate for a celebration of the birth of Jesus.

The Festival of Saturnalia took place around December 25th, so the Roman Emperor Constantine chose to replace that festival with Christmas. This occurred during the fourth century AD. Saint Augustine introduced Christmas Day to the British Isles in the sixth century AD.

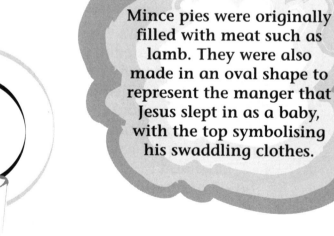

Mince pies were originally filled with meat such as lamb. They were also made in an oval shape to represent the manger that Jesus slept in as a baby, with the top symbolising his swaddling clothes.

The name "Christmas" comes from the Mass of Christ. A Mass (otherwise known as a Communion Service, Eucharist or Lord's Supper) is the service at which Christ's death is remembered through the symbols of bread and wine. The name Christ-Mass was shortened to Christmas.

The custom of sending Christmas cards started in England in 1843. The man responsible was Sir Henry Cole, a civil servant interested in the new "Public Post Office". He was concerned to find ways that ordinary people could use this service and came up with the idea of Christmas cards. With his friend John Horsley, an artist, he designed the first card and sold it for one shilling.

Boxing Day takes place on December 26th. It is celebrated in only a few countries. It began in England during the Middle Ages. Boxing Day was the day when the alms boxes were opened in parish churches so that the contents could be distributed to the poor.

The first cards usually had pictures of the Nativity. In late Victorian times, robins became popular because the postmen were nicknamed "Robin Postmen" on account of the red uniforms they wore.

Mistletoe is a plant that grows on willow and apple trees. The practice of hanging it in one's home originates in the days of the druids. Mistletoe was thought to possess mystical powers that would ward off evil spirits. It was also used as a sign of friendship. This is where the custom of kissing under mistletoe comes from, a custom that originated once again in England. A berry would be picked from the sprig of mistletoe before the person could be kissed. When all the berries had gone, there would be no more kissing!!

Holly and ivy were originally used in pre-Christian times as well. Like mistletoe, they were thought to be associated with warding off evil powers. They were used in the celebration of the Winter Solstice Festival.

When Christianity came to Western Europe, the holly and the ivy were turned into Christian symbols and used in Christmas celebrations. Christian meanings were attributed to these symbols:

The prickly leaves of the holly were thought to symbolise the crown of thorns.

The berries were seen to represent the drops of blood shed by Jesus because of the thorns.

Ivy has to cling to something. This is seen to symbolise our need to depend on God.

The first Christmas crackers were made in 1850 by a London sweetmaker. His name was Tom Smith. One evening, while he was sitting in front of his log fire, Smith became engrossed in the sparks and cracking sounds coming from the hearth. Suddenly it occurred to him what fun it would be if his sweets and toys could be opened with a cracking sound as the decorative wrappers were pulled in half.

The first nativity scene dates back to 1223, when Francis of Assisi recreated the scene of Christ's birth in the town of Greccio. St Francis was worried that ordinary people had no real grasp of what had happened at Christ's birth. So he secured the assistance of a rich patron and set about recreating the original scene. He used a life-size figure of the Christ-child, live animals, a manger, straw and so forth. He and his friends played the parts of Joseph, Mary, the shepherds, and the Magi. Worshippers flocked to this nativity scene. St Francis had managed to portray the birth of Christ in all its humility rather than with the pomp and splendour of his day.

The modern Christmas tree dates from the 8th century, when Saint Boniface was converting the Germanic tribes. The tribes worshipped oak trees, decorating them for the winter solstice. Boniface cut down an enormous oak tree that was central to the worship of a particular tribe, but a fir tree grew in its place. The evergreen was offered as a symbol of Christianity, which the newly converted Germans began decorating for Christmas. Prince Albert, who was German, introduced the Christmas tree to England after his marriage to Queen Victoria in 1840. German immigrants to Pennsylvania brought Christmas trees to America.

O Christmas Tree! O Christmas Tree!
How richly God has decked thee!
O Christmas Tree! O Christmas Tree!
How richly God has decked thee!
Thou bidst us true and faithful be,
And trust in God unchangingly.
O Christmas Tree! O Christmas Tree!
How richly God has decked thee!

P is for Peace

For a child is born to us, a son is given to us. And the government will rest on his shoulders. These will be his royal titles: Wonderful Counsellor, Mighty God, Everlasting Father, Prince of Peace. (Isaiah 9:6)

Christmas has always been a time when people have been more open to forgetting their differences and being reconciled, whether at the level of family or of nations. Who can forget the First World War, when British and German soldiers laid down their arms and came out into No Man's Land to play a game of football on Christmas Day? The birth of Jesus Christ was greeted with the angels declaring "peace on earth". Every Christmas we are reminded that true peace is found in Jesus Christ – the Prince of Peace.

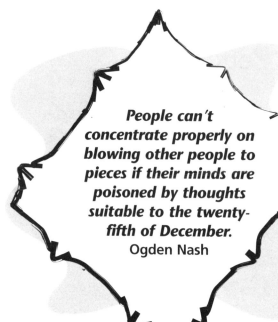

People can't concentrate properly on blowing other people to pieces if their minds are poisoned by thoughts suitable to the twenty-fifth of December.
Ogden Nash

I do like Christmas on the whole ... In its clumsy way, it does approach Peace and Goodwill. But it is clumsier every year.
E M Forster

Our trouble is we want the peace without the Prince.
Addison Leitch

Henry Wadsworth Longfellow was filled with sorrow at the tragic death of his wife in a fire in 1861. The Civil War broke out the same year, and it seemed this was an additional punishment. Two years later, Longfellow was again saddened to learn that his son had been seriously wounded in the Army of the Potomac.

Sitting down at his desk, one Christmas Day, he heard the church bells ringing. It was in this setting that Longfellow wrote these lines:

I heard the bells on Christmas Day
Their old familiar carols play,
And wild and sweet
The words repeat
Of peace on earth, goodwill to men!

And in despair I bowed my head;
"There is no peace on earth," I said;
"For hate is strong
And mocks the song
Of peace on earth, goodwill to men."

Then pealed the bells more loud and deep.
"God is not dead, nor doth he sleep!
The wrong shall fail,
The right prevail,
With peace on earth, goodwill to men!"

During the Second World War, the Allied Army was advancing through France. The Germans were making a last stand wherever they could. During a night of heavy fog the opposing armies moved very close. Only a long green meadow and one farmhouse separated them.

As dawn came, the fog lifted. Bullets and bombs began to explode, and men began to die. After a long period of severe battle, the house in the green meadow was hit and began to burn. Then someone whispered, "Look!" It was unbelievable, but there was a *small baby* crawling across the field.

As the soldiers saw the child, the shooting stopped. It became very still. Every eye was on the baby.

Suddenly, a soldier got up from his position, ran out into the open, grabbed the baby up in his arms, and ran back to his line. In a moment a great cheer went up on both sides, and the bullets began to fly again.

The baby brought peace just for a moment.

"May the forgiving spirit of Him to whom we dedicate this season prevail again on earth.
May hunger disappear and terrorists cease their senseless acts.
May people live in freedom, worshipping as they see fit, loving others.
May the sanctity of the home be ever preserved.
May peace, everlasting peace, reign supreme."

A former president of the Norwegian Academy of Sciences and historians from England, Egypt, Germany, and India have come up with some startling information: since 3600 BC the world has known only 292 years of peace! During this period there have been 14,351 wars, large and small, in which 3.64 billion people have been killed. The value of the property destroyed would pay for a golden belt around the world 97.2 miles wide and 33 feet thick. Since 650 BC there have also been 1,656 arms races, only 16 of which have not ended in war. The remainder ended in the economic collapse of the countries involved.

Advent was one week away, so a family thought they'd see what the kids remembered from the previous year's celebrations.

"Who can tell me what the four candles in the Advent wreath represent?" the father asked.

His son jumped in with seven-year-old wisdom, saying, "There's love, joy, peace and ..."

At that moment the daughter interrupted, "Peace and QUIET!"

For lo! the days are hastening on,
By prophet-bards foretold,
When, with the ever-circling years,
Comes round the age of gold;
When peace shall over all the earth
Its ancient splendours fling,
And the whole world send back the song
Which now the angels sing.

Q is for Queues

They ran to the village and found Mary and Joseph. And there was the baby, lying in the manger. (Luke 2:16)

Christian painters have traditionally depicted the birth of Jesus Christ as an extremely crowded event. The shepherds and the wise men jostle with the parents, not to mention the animals, to catch a glimpse of the baby Jesus. In reality, of course, the scene was far from like this. We simply don't know how many shepherds there were, or wise men for that matter. It is also certain that the wise men arrived at a different time from the shepherds, maybe up to two years later. The crowded nativity scene is therefore most likely a fiction. Nevertheless, it does function as something of an ancient counterpart to our modern phenomenon of queuing up to see and to acquire during Christmas shopping. It also points to our inability to live without noise, hurry and crowds.

It was just a few days before Christmas, when two men decided to go sailing while their wives went Christmas shopping. While the men were sailing a storm came up – a mighty storm that tossed the boat back and forth across the water. Finally, the tiny sailboat was forced upon the shore of a small island. The men jumped out of the boat and tried to push it back into the water. Suddenly, they realised they were being fired upon by the island's hostile natives. As they dodged poisonous darts, standing waist-deep in freezing water in the middle of a storm, one said to the other,

"I realise that today hasn't exactly gone as planned, but this sure beats Christmas shopping, doesn't it?!"

It was the week before Christmas. Parking spaces were hard to come by. There were long lines, crowded stores, rude people, and grossly inflated prices. In one long checkout line, one man was heard to say, "They should kill the guy who started Christmas." One wise and godly woman in the line said, "They did – they hung Him on a cross." Therein lies the REAL Christmas story.

Once again we find ourselves enmeshed in the Holiday Season, that very special time of year when we join with our loved ones in sharing centuries-old traditions such as trying to find a parking space at the mall. We traditionally do this in my family by driving around the parking lot until we see a shopper emerge from the mall, then we follow her – in very much the same spirit as the Three Wise Men, who 2,000 years ago followed a star, week after week, until it led them to a parking space.

Dave Barry

The way we observe Christmas these days is a far cry from the tranquil manger scene that welcomed Christ into the world some 2,000 years ago. Consider the contrasts of:

- The solitude of the manger versus today's Christmas rush
- God's mercy in sending his Son versus the rudeness and selfishness of holiday shoppers
- The free gift of salvation versus the forced giving of commercialisation
- The adoration of the newborn King versus commitments that distract us from worship
- The joyful anticipation of the shepherds versus the dread of the holiday hoopla.

Unfortunately, this holy season has become something of a gift-buying marathon. Some people go into debt to buy costly gifts they can't afford and their families don't need. The result is debt, stress, and worry.

We need to move away from the materialism of December and shift our emphasis from the shopping trolley back to the manger as the reason for the season. Christmas isn't the time to throw caution to the wind and allow a well-meaning, generous spirit to dictate spending. Instead, it's the time to honour the One whose birthday we're celebrating and be good financial stewards of all he has entrusted to us.

Howard Dayton

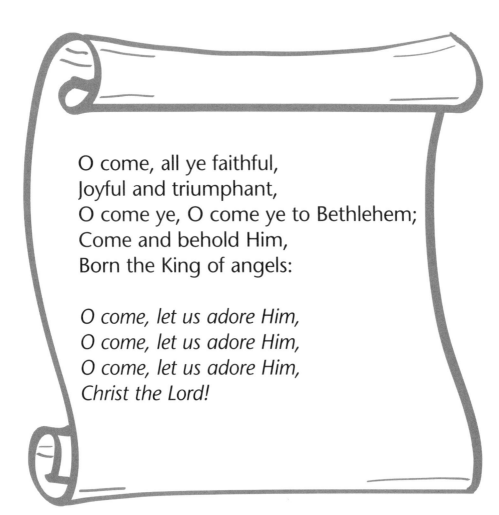

O come, all ye faithful,
Joyful and triumphant,
O come ye, O come ye to Bethlehem;
Come and behold Him,
Born the King of angels:

O come, let us adore Him,
O come, let us adore Him,
O come, let us adore Him,
Christ the Lord!

R is for Revelling

Suddenly, the angel was joined by a vast host of others – the armies of heaven – praising God:

> *"Glory to God in the highest heaven,*
> *and peace on earth to all whom God favours."*

(Luke 2:13–14)

The first Christmas was the occasion for great rejoicing. Heaven joined in the party as the Saviour was born in Bethlehem. Today, of course, the rejoicing is no longer related for most people to the birth of Jesus. It is motivated by the joy of having days off work and the excesses of food and drink. Even during working hours the office party has become the focal point of the Christmas celebrations. Today, even our children now associate Christmas not with Jesus but with parties, balloons, crackers, presents and food. Perhaps we have returned to the pagan revelling that characterised our nation's life before Christianity.

Most people gain around 5lbs over Christmas, having consumed 6,000 calories on Christmas Day alone.

On the FIRST day of Christmas this is what I ate: a scrumptious piece of chocolate Christmas cake.

On the SECOND day of Christmas this is what I ate: two mince pies and a scrumptious piece of chocolate Christmas cake.

On the THIRD day of Christmas this is what I ate: three sausage rolls, two mince pies and a scrumptious piece of chocolate Christmas cake.

On the FOURTH day of Christmas this is what I ate: four roasted spuds, three sausage rolls, two mince pies and a scrumptious piece of chocolate Christmas cake.

On the FIFTH day of Christmas this is what I ate: five Christmas puuuuuuuuds, four roasted spuds, three sausage rolls, two mince pies and a scrumptious piece of chocolate Christmas cake.

On the SIXTH day of Christmas this is what I ate: six balls of stuffing, five Christmas puuuuuuuuds, four roasted spuds, three sausage rolls, two mince pies and a scrumptious piece of chocolate Christmas cake.

On the SEVENTH day of Christmas this is what I ate: seven chipolatas, six balls of stuffing, five Christmas puuuuuuuuds, four roasted spuds, three sausage rolls, two mince pies and a scrumptious piece of chocolate Christmas cake.

On the EIGHTH day of Christmas this is what I ate: eight brandy butters, seven chipolatas, six balls of stuffing, five Christmas puuuuuuuuds, four roasted spuds, three sausage rolls, two mince pies and a scrumptious piece of chocolate Christmas cake.

On the NINTH day of Christmas this is what I ate: nine Brussels sprouts, eight brandy butters, seven chipolatas, six balls of stuffing, five Christmas puuuuuuuuds, four roasted spuds, three sausage rolls, two mince pies and a scrumptious piece of chocolate Christmas cake.

On the TENTH day of Christmas this is what I ate: ten cheesy crackers, nine Brussels sprouts, eight brandy butters, seven chipolatas, six balls of stuffing, five Christmas puuuuuuuuds, four roasted spuds, three sausage rolls, two mince pies and a scrumptious piece of chocolate Christmas cake.

On the ELEVENTH day of Christmas this is what I ate: eleven plates of turkey, ten cheesy crackers, nine Brussels sprouts, eight brandy butters, seven chipolatas, six balls of stuffing, five Christmas puuuuuuuuds, four roasted spuds, three sausage rolls, two mince pies and a scrumptious piece of chocolate Christmas cake.

On the TWELFTH day of Christmas this is what I ate: twelve chocolate Santas, eleven plates of turkey, ten cheesy crackers, nine Brussels sprouts, eight brandy butters, seven chipolatas, six balls of stuffing, five Christmas puuuuuuuuds, four roasted spuds, three sausage rolls, two mince pies and a scrumptious piece of chocolate Christmas cake.

> Oh look, yet another Christmas TV special! How touching to have the meaning of Christmas brought to us by cola, fast food and beer ... Who'd have ever guessed that product consumption, popular entertainment and spirituality would mix so harmoniously?
> **Bill Watterson, Calvin & Hobbes**

FROM: Pat Smith, Human Resources Director

TO: Everyone
DATE: December 1
RE: Christmas Party

I'm happy to inform you that the company Christmas Party will take place on December 23, starting at noon in the banquet room at Luigi's Open Pit Barbecue. No-host bar, but plenty of eggnog! We'll have a small band playing traditional carols … feel free to sing along. And don't be surprised if our CEO shows up dressed as Santa Claus!

∽◌◌◌∾

FROM: Pat Smith, Human Resources Director
DATE: December 2
RE: Christmas Party

In no way was yesterday's memo intended to exclude our Jewish employees.
      We recognise that Chanukah is an important holiday which often coincides with Christmas, though unfortunately not this year. However, from now on we're calling it our "Holiday Party". The same policy applies to employees who are celebrating Kwanzaa at this time. Happy now?

∽◌◌◌∾

FROM: Pat Smith, Human Resources Director
DATE: December 3
RE: Holiday Party

Regarding the note I received from a member of Alcoholics Anonymous requesting a non-drinking table … you didn't sign your name. I'm happy to accommodate this request, but if I put a sign on a table that reads,"AA Only", you wouldn't be anonymous any more. How am I supposed to handle this? Somebody?

∽◌◌◌∾

FROM: Pat Smith, Human Resources Director
DATE: December 7
RE: Holiday Party

What a diverse company we are! I had no idea that December 20 begins the Muslim holy month of Ramadan, which forbids eating, drinking and intimacy during daylight hours. There goes the party! Seriously, we can appreciate how a luncheon this time of year does not accommodate our Muslim employees' beliefs. Perhaps Luigi's can hold off on serving your meal until the end of the party. The days are so short this time of year – or else package everything for take-home in little foil swans. Will that work?
      Meanwhile, I've arranged for members of Overeaters Anonymous

to sit farthest from the dessert buffet and pregnant women will get the table closest to the restrooms. Did I miss anything?

∽⊙∾

FROM: Pat Smith, Human Resources Director
DATE: December 8
RE: Holiday Party

So December 22 marks the Winter Solstice … What do you expect me to do, a tap dance on your heads? Fire regulations at Luigi's prohibit the burning of sage by our "earth-based goddess-worshipping" employees, but we'll try to accommodate your shamanic drumming circle during the band's breaks.
    Okay???

∽⊙∾

FROM: Pat Smith, Human Resources Director
DATE: December 9
RE: Holiday Party

People, people, nothing sinister was intended by having our CEO dress up like Santa Claus! Even if the anagram of "Santa" does happen to be Satan, there is no evil connotation to our own "little man in a red suit".
    It's a tradition, folks, like sugar shock at Hallowe'en or family feuds over the Thanksgiving turkey or broken hearts on Valentine's Day. Could we lighten up?

∽⊙∾

FROM: Karen Jones, Acting Human Resources Director
DATE: December 14
RE: Pat Smith and Holiday Party

I'm sure I speak for all of us in wishing Pat Smith a speedy recovery from her stress-related illness, and I'll continue to forward your cards to her at the sanatorium. In the meantime, management has decided to cancel our Holiday Party and give everyone the afternoon of the 23rd off with full pay. Happy Chanuk-Kwanzaa-Solsti-Rama-Mas at this time.

∽⊙∾

The average person will gain six pounds during the Christmas season.

Here is the adult analysis of Christmas eating:

- If you eat something and no one sees you eat it, it has no calories.
- If you drink a diet drink with chocolate, the calories in the chocolate bar are cancelled by the diet drink.
- When you eat with someone else, calories don't count if you don't eat more than they do.
- Food used for medicinal purposes never counts; that's just mulled wine, sherry and a little brandy.
- If you fatten everyone else around you, you'll look thinner.
- Biscuit pieces and crumbs contain no calories; the process of breaking causes calorie leakage.
- Things licked off spoons have no calories, especially home-made brandy butter.
- Foods with similar colouring have the same calories, i.e. turkey and white chocolate.

Christmas begins about the first of December with an office party and ends when you finally realise what you spent, around April fifteenth of the next year.

P J O'Rourke

A Christmas List

Fear less, hope more;
Eat less, chew more;
Whine less, breathe more;
Talk less, say more;
Hate less, love more;
And all good things will be yours.

The way you spend Christmas is far more important than how much.
Henry David Thoreau

Good King Wenceslas rings up a local pizza restaurant to order a pizza.

"Certainly your Majesty," says the manager, "will it be your usual? Deep pan, crisp and even?"

I will honour Christmas in my heart, and try to keep it all the year.
Charles Dickens
(A Christmas Carol)

Lt Gerald Coffee spent seven years as a POW during the Vietnam War. During his second Christmas in camp he made an amazing discovery. He had been stripped of everything by which he measured his identity: rank, uniform, family, money. Alone, in a cramped 3' x 7' cell, he began to understand the significance of Christmas. Removed from all commercial distractions, he was able to focus on the simplicity of Christ's birth. Although he was lonely and afraid, he realised that this Christmas could be his most meaningful, because now, more than ever before, he understood the event.

assailing is one of those activities, like singing "E-o-e-o-e-o", that we only ever encounter in the Christmas season, and which, frankly, not many people really understand. As far as I can discover, wassailing derives from Anglo-Saxon ceremonial health-drinking, with the toast "Waes Hael!", which means "Good health!", or, "You're my besht mate, you are, I'll never forget you ..." or other similar sentiments.

You may be wondering what it was that people quaffed while out a-wassailing in the era before Bacardi Breezers. Wassail punch is essentially mulled ale.

Catherine Fox

Recipe For Christmas Joy

Ingredients
- 1/2 cup Hugs
- 4 tsp Kisses
- 2 cups Smiles
- 4 cups Love
- 1 cup Special Holiday Cheer
- 1/2 cup Peace on Earth
- 3 tsp Christmas Spirit
- 2 cups Goodwill Towards Men
- 1 Sprig of Mistletoe
- 1 medium-size bag of Christmas Snowflakes (the regular kind won't do!)

Method
Mix Hugs, Kisses, Smiles and Love until consistent. Blend in Holiday Cheer, Peace on Earth, Christmas Spirit and the Good Will Towards Men. Use the mixture to fill a large, warm heart, where it can be stored for a lifetime. (It never goes bad!) Serve as desired under mistletoe, sprinkled liberally with special Christmas Snowflakes. It is especially good when accompanied by Christmas carols and family get-togethers. Serve to one and all.

"Bring me flesh, and bring me wine,
Bring me pine logs hither:
Thou and I will see him dine,
When we bear them thither."
Page and monarch, forth they went,
Forth they went together;
Thro' the rude wind's wild lament
And the bitter weather.

S is for Santa

Most people today associate Christmas with Santa Claus. In December 2003, the Churches Advertising Network (CAN) issued a series of posters and adverts depicting a traditional nativity scene. But instead of the baby Jesus lying in the manger the pictures portrayed an infant Santa (in full regalia). The motto of the campaign was simply "Ask him for something".

The origins of Santa Claus are complex, but they lie at least in part in the figure of Saint Nicholas.

Saint Nicholas was the bishop of the Mediterranean city of Myra. He was born to rich parents in Patara in about 270 AD. His parents died when he was young and he was left a fortune. As a young man, Nicholas heard about a family that was starving. Under the cover of night, Nicholas threw a bag of gold coins through the window of their humble dwelling.

Nicholas became a minister and was eventually made bishop of Myra. He led his churches through one of the worst times of persecution in Christian history. In AD 303, the Roman Emperor Diocletian ordered a brutal attack on all Christians. Those suspected of being followers of Jesus were ordered to make sacrifices to pagan gods. Nicholas and thousands of others refused.

Ministers, bishops and lay people were dragged to prison and tortured. Believers were executed in horrible and public ways. Yet persecution did not triumph. Christians who survived this time were called "saints" or "confessors" because they kept on confessing that Jesus is Lord. Nicholas was one of these.

Finally, Bishop Nicholas came out of prison, freed by a decree of the new Emperor Constantine (who had become a Christian). As Nicholas returned to Myra, his people came out and shouted, "Nicholas! Confessor! Saint Nicholas has come home!"

Saint Nicholas served as bishop in Myra for another 30 years. Through his ministry, thousands found salvation and healing. Nicholas died on December 6, about 343 AD, and his death was mourned by everyone in the city.

Santa Claus of yuletide tradition still has some echoes of this great saint. The colour of his outfit recollects the red of the bishop's robes. Gifts secretly brought on Christmas Eve remind us of his generosity to the poor.

While many people think that Christmas is all about Santa, it is in reality about Jesus. When you consider the differences between Santa and Jesus – not to mention the fact that Santa is based on a Christian saint! – the folly is exposed. Consider, for example, the following contrasts:

Santa lives at the North Pole … JESUS is everywhere.

Santa rides in a sleigh … JESUS rides on the wind and walks on the water.

Santa comes but once a year … JESUS is an ever-present help.

Santa fills your stocking … JESUS supplies all your needs.

Santa comes down your chimney uninvited … JESUS stands at your door and knocks, and then enters your heart when invited.

You have to wait in line to see Santa … JESUS is as close as the mention of His name.

Santa lets you sit on his lap … JESUS lets you rest in His arms.

Santa doesn't know your name; all he can say is "Hi, little boy or girl, what's your name?" … JESUS knew our name before we did. Not only does He know our name, He knows our address too. He knows our history and future He even knows how many hairs are on our heads.

Santa has a belly like a bowl full of jelly … JESUS has a heart full of love.

All Santa can offer is HO HO HO … JESUS offers health, help and hope.

Santa says "You better not cry" … JESUS says "Cast all your cares on me for I care for you."

Santa's little helpers make toys … JESUS makes new life, mends wounded hearts, repairs broken homes and builds mansions.

Santa may make you chuckle but … JESUS gives you joy that is your strength.

While Santa puts gifts under your tree … JESUS became our gift and died on a tree.

It's obvious there is really no comparison. We need to remember WHO Christmas is all about. We need to put *Christ* back in *Christ*mas, Jesus is still the reason for the season. Yes, Jesus is better, he is even better than Santa Claus.

The three stages of a man's life:

1. **He believes in Santa Claus;**
2. **He doesn't believe in Santa Claus;**
3. **He *is* Santa Claus.**

Reasons why Santa Claus has to be a woman!

- Men can't pack a bag
- Men would rather be dead than caught wearing red velvet
- Men don't answer their mail
- Men aren't interested in stockings unless somebody's wearing them
- Men don't think about getting gifts till Christmas Eve, when it's too late
- Men refuse to stop and ask for directions when they get lost
- Finally, being responsible for Christmas would require a commitment.

Does Santa call his elves "subordinate clauses"?

Doug Hecox

As a little girl climbed onto Santa's lap, Santa asked the usual: "And what would you like for Christmas?"

The child stared at him open-mouthed and horrified for a minute, then gasped: "Didn't you get my E-mail?"

Let me see if I've got this Santa business straight. You say he wears a beard, has no discernible source of income and flies to cities all over the world under cover of darkness? You sure this guy isn't laundering illegal drug money?

Tom Armstrong

I stopped believing in Santa Claus when I was six. Mother took me to see him in a department store and he asked for my autograph.

Shirley Temple

I never believed in Santa Claus because I knew no white man would be coming into my neighbourhood after dark.

Dick Gregory

I played Santa Claus many times, and if you don't believe it, check out the divorce settlements awarded my wives.

Groucho Marx

Santa Claus has the right idea. Visit people once a year.

Victor Borge

Santa Claus wears a red suit: he must be a communist. And a beard and long hair: must be a pacifist. What's in that pipe that he's smoking?

Arlo Guthrie

Santa is even-tempered. Santa does not hit children over the head who kick him. Santa uses the term "folks" rather than "Mummy and Daddy" because of all the broken homes. Santa does not have a three-martini lunch. Santa does not borrow money from store employees. Santa wears a good deodorant.

Jenny Zink *(To employees of Western Temporary Services, world's largest supplier of Santa Clauses, NY Times 21 November 1984.)*

A Santa figure measuring 15.6 metres high, 11 metres wide and 4 metres deep stood at the entrance of the Tanglin Mall, Singapore, from 10th November 1996 till 3rd January 1997. It weighed 2.5 tonnes and was constructred from polyfoam and metal.

The deepest ho-ho-ho was performed by David Broughton Davies at the Santathon event held at Westway Leisure Centre, London, on 6th December 2001. The reading was taken at a low frequency over three attempts and measured 55.9 decibels.

The world's largest gathering of Santas occurred on 7th December 2002, when 2,865 costumed Santas paraded down the streets of Bralanda, Sweden. All participants wore red Santa costumes with matching hats and fake white beards.

Oh, jingle bells, jingle bells,
jingle all the way,
Oh what fun it is to ride
In a one-horse open sleigh.
Jingle bells, jingle bells,
Jingle all the way,
Oh what fun it is to ride
In a one-horse open sleigh.

T is for Thanksgiving

Thanks be to God for his indescribable gift! (2 Corinthians 9:15)

Christmas is a time when we should excel in the gratitude attitude. Someone once said that human beings are at their best when they are thankful. Shakespeare's King Lear said that it was sharper than a serpent's tooth to have a thankless child. Thanksgiving is therefore as much a part of Christmas as anything else. Yet how difficult it is to persuade children to engage in the discipline of writing thank-you letters after they have opened their presents! Christmas is a time for taking the time to thank God for his great gift of Jesus Christ, and one another for the gifts that we receive.

Gluttony and surfeiting are no proper occasions for thanksgiving.
Charles Lamb, 1821

When we were children we were grateful to those who filled our stockings with toys at Christmastime. Why are we not grateful to God for filling our stockings with legs?

G K Chesterton

A four-year-old boy was asked to give thanks before Christmas dinner. The family members bowed their heads in expectation. He began his prayer, thanking God for all his friends, naming them one by one. Then he thanked God for Mummy, Daddy, brother, sister, Grandma, Grandpa, and all his aunts and uncles. Then he began to thank God for the food.

He gave thanks for the turkey, the dressing, the fruit salad, the cranberry sauce, the pies, the cakes, even the Cool Whip. Then he paused, and everyone waited – and waited. After a long silence, the young fellow looked up at his mother and asked, "If I thank God for the broccoli, won't he know that I'm lying?"

Helen Aberg used to give generous Christmas presents to her several grandchildren, but the kids never sent thank-you letters, despite the urgings of their respective parents. But then, one year, things changed. Grandma sent a hundred dollar Christmas cheque to each grandchild. The very next day, each child came over in person to thank her. She was telling this to a friend of hers, who said, "How wonderful! What do you think caused them to become so polite?"

"Oh," said Helen, "it was easy. This year I didn't sign the cheques."

What follows is perhaps the ultimate example of a Christmas thank-you letter, composed around the "Twelve Days of Christmas":

My dearest darling Edward, Dec. 25

What a wonderful surprise has just greeted me! That sweet partridge, in that lovely little pear-tree; what an enchanting, romantic, poetic present! Bless you, and thank you.

Your deeply loving Emily

《∞》

Beloved Edward, Dec. 26
The two turtle-doves arrived this morning, and are cooing away in the pear-tree as I write. I'm so touched and grateful!

With undying love, as always, Emily

《∞》

My darling Edward, Dec. 27

You do think of the most original presents! Who ever thought of sending anybody three French hens? Do they really come all the way from France? It's a pity we have no chicken coops, but I expect we'll find some. Anyway, thank you so much; they're lovely.

Your devoted Emily

《∞》

Dearest Edward, Dec. 28

What a surprise! Four calling birds arrived this morning. They are very sweet, even if they do call rather loudly – they make telephoning almost impossible – but I expect they'll calm down when they get used to their new home. Anyway, I'm very grateful, of course I am.

Love from Emily

《∞》

Dearest Edward, Dec. 29

The mailman has just delivered five most beautiful gold rings, one for each finger, and all fitting perfectly! A really lovely present! Lovelier, in a way, than birds, which do take rather a lot of looking after. The four that arrived yesterday are still making a terrible row, and I'm afraid none of us got much sleep last night. Mother says she wants to use the rings to "wring" their necks. Mother has such a sense of humour. This time she's only joking, I think, but I do know what she means. Still, I love the rings.

Bless you, Emily

《∞》

Dear Edward, Dec. 30

Whatever I expected to find when I opened the front door this morning, it certainly wasn't six socking great geese laying eggs all over the porch. Frankly, I rather hoped that you had stopped sending me birds. We have no room for them, and they've already ruined the croquet lawn. I know you meant well, but let's call a halt, shall we?

Love, Emily

《∞》

Edward, Dec. 31

I thought I said NO MORE BIRDS. This morning I woke up to find no more than seven swans, all trying to get into our tiny goldfish pond. I'd rather not think what's happened to the goldfish. The whole house seems to be full of birds, to say nothing of what they leave behind them, so please, please, stop!

Your Emily

《∞》

Jan. 1

Frankly, I prefer the birds. What am I to do with eight milkmaids? And their cows! Is this some kind of a joke? If so, I'm afraid I don't find it very amusing.

Emily

《∞》

Look here, Edward, Jan. 2

This has gone far enough. You say you're sending me nine ladies dancing. All I can say is, judging from the way they dance, they're certainly not ladies. If you value our friendship, which I do (less and less), kindly stop this ridiculous behaviour at once!

Emily

《∞》

Jan. 3

As I write this letter, ten old men are prancing up and down all over what used to be the garden, before the geese and the swans and the cows got at it.

Meanwhile the neighbours are trying to have us evicted. I shall never speak to you again.

Emily

《∞》

Jan. 4

This is the last straw! You know I detest bagpipes! The place has now become something between a menagerie and a madhouse, and a man from the council has just declared it unfit for habitation. At least Mother has been spared this last outrage; they took her away yesterday afternoon in an ambulance. I hope you're satisfied.

《∞》

Jan. 5

Sir,

Our client, Miss Emily Wilbraham, instructs me to inform you
that with the arrival on her premises at 7:30 this morning of
the entire percussion section of the London Symphony
Orchestra, and several of their friends, she has no course
left open to her but to seek an injunction to prevent you
importuning her further. I am making arrangements for the
return of much assorted livestock.

I am, Sir, yours faithfully,

G Creep, Lawyer acting on behalf of Miss Wilbraham

《∞》

The minister of a city church enjoyed a drink now and then, but his passion was for peach brandy. One of his congregants would make him a bottle each Christmas. One year, when the minister went to visit his friend, hoping for his usual Christmas present, he was not disappointed, but his friend told him that he had to thank him for the peach brandy from the pulpit the next Sunday.

In his haste to get the bottle, the minister hurriedly agreed and left. So, the next Sunday the minister suddenly remembered that he had to make a public announcement that he was being supplied with alcohol by a member of the church. That morning, his friend sat in the church with a grin on his face, waiting to see the minister's embarrassment.

The minister climbed into the pulpit and said, "Before we begin, I have an announcement. I would very much like to thank my friend, Joe, for his kind gift of peaches … and for the spirit in which they were given!"

The very purpose of Christ's coming into the world was that He might offer up His life as a sacrifice for the sins of men. He came to die. This is the heart of Christmas.
Billy Graham

It's Christmas time at our house and we're putting up a tree.
I wish I could find some simple way to remember God's gift to me.

Some little sign or symbol, to show friends stopping by,
The little babe was born one day, but He really came to die.

Some symbol of His nail-pierced hands, the blood He shed for me.
What if I hung a nail on my Christmas tree?

I know it was His love for us, that held Him to a tree,
But when I see this simple nail, I'll know He died for me.

It may seem strange at Christmas time, to think of nails and wood,
But both were used in Jesus' life to bring us something good.

From manger bed, to crown of thorns, to death on Calvary,
God used the wood and nails of men to set all people free.

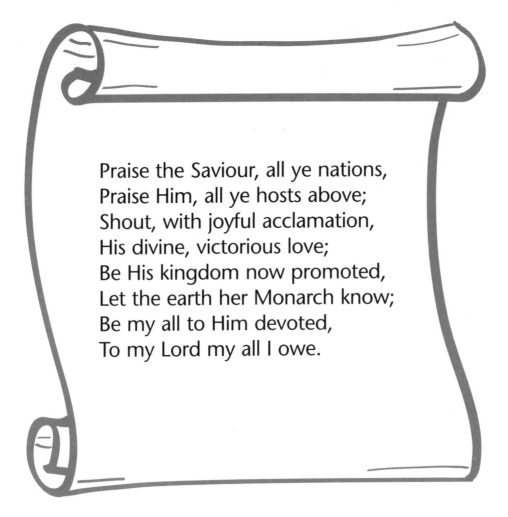

Praise the Saviour, all ye nations,
Praise Him, all ye hosts above;
Shout, with joyful acclamation,
His divine, victorious love;
Be His kingdom now promoted,
Let the earth her Monarch know;
Be my all to Him devoted,
To my Lord my all I owe.

U is for Unselfishness

I want you to share your food with the hungry and to welcome poor wanderers into your homes. Give clothes to those who need them, and do not hide from relatives who need your help. (Isaiah 58:7)

As a festival, Christmas is not mentioned in the Bible at all. The major festivals that God instituted were the three festivals that required pilgrimage to Jerusalem: Passover, Pentecost and Tabernacles. In these and other biblical festivals, provision was always made for the poor. Would that the same were true of Christmas! Instead of thinking of others – especially the poor – most people think only of themselves. As the saying goes, the smallest Christmas present is a person wrapped up in themselves. The challenge of Christmas is the challenge to put others before ourselves and, in the simple words of the Bible, "remember the poor". As someone has written:

> *Now that the song of the angels is stilled*
> *Now that the star in the sky is gone*
> *Now that kings and princes are home*
> *Now that shepherds are back with their flocks*
> *the work of Christmas begins:*
> *to find the lost*
> *to heal the broken*
> *to feed the hungry*
> *to release the prisoner*
> *to rebuild the nations*
> *to bring peace among the people*
> *to make music in the heart.*

One of the best definitions of poverty comes from Archbishop Oscar Romero, who places poverty in the context of Christmas for us:

No one can celebrate a genuine Christmas without being truly poor. The self-sufficient, the proud, those who, because they have everything, look down on others, those who have no need even of God – for them there will be no Christmas. Only the poor, the hungry, those who need someone to come on their behalf, will have that someone. That someone is God, Emmanuel, God-with-us. Without poverty of spirit there can be no abundance of God.

"At this festive season of the year, Mr Scrooge," said the gentleman, taking up a pen, "it is more than usually desirable that we should make some slight provision for the poor and destitute, who suffer greatly at the present time ... We choose this time, because it is a time, of all others, when Want is keenly felt, and Abundance rejoices."
Charles Dickens
(*A Christmas Carol*)

One little boy wrote the following letter to Santa:

Dear Santa,
There are three little boys who live at our house.
There's Jeffrey. He's two.
There's David. He's four.
There's Norman. He is seven.
Jeffrey is good some of the time.
David is good some of the time.
Norman is good all of the time.
I am Norman.

I gave a Christmas tea party this afternoon, at three.
Twas very small, three guests in all – I, myself, and me.
Myself ate all the sandwiches while I drank all the tea.
Twas also I who ate the pie and passed the cake to me.

Don't expect too much of Christmas Day. You can't crowd into it any arrears of unselfishness and kindliness that may have accrued during the past twelve months.
Oren Arnold

This Christmas, why not live simply, so that others may simply live?
J John

A Christmas candle is a lovely thing;
It makes no noise at all,
But softly gives itself away;
While quite unselfish, it grows small.
Eva K Logue

Christmas is a season of joy and goodwill, of singing and merriment and of generosity. Christmas is a season of sharing and love. Christmas is a season of concern for the needs of others, a season of the helping hand. And that's as it should be. For there is great satisfaction in making others happy.
Salvation Army, *War Cry*

I sometimes think we expect too much of Christmas Day. We try to crowd into it the long arrears of kindliness and humanity of the whole year. As for me, I like to take my Christmas a little at a time, all through the year. And thus I drift along into the holidays – let them overtake me unexpectedly – waking up some fine morning and suddenly saying to myself: "Why, this is Christmas Day!"

David Grayson

"Somehow he, Tim, gets thoughtful sitting by himself so much, and thinks the strangest things you ever heard. He told me, coming home, that he hoped the people saw him in the church, because he was a cripple, and it might be pleasant for them to remember upon Christmas Day, who made lame beggars walk, and blind men see."

Charles Dickens (*A Christmas Carol*)

A CHRISTMAS ANGEL

It was a bright Christmas morning and after travelling all through the night my exhausted family and I pulled in to a small diner for breakfast. My husband and my son were the only family in the place.

I heard my 18-month-old Sammy shout with glee, "Hi there …" His fat baby hands banged the back of his chair. "Hi there." His face was alive with excitement and he grinned from ear to ear.

I stretched my neck to see what was causing my son so much joy and I could scarce take it in.

There he stood, filthy, greasy and worn, with a wrinkled, weathered face.

"Hi there, baby boy."

My husband and I exchanged a look that was a cross between "What do we do?" and "Poor soul".

Our meal arrived and we tried to settle Sammy, but he fussed as the street person shouted across the room, "Do you know peek a boo … PEEK A BOO, little boy."

Sammy kept laughing and trying to talk to the man.

Nobody thought this was cute. The guy was obviously drunk and an embarrassment. My husband wolfed down his food, headed for the door and then said tensely, "Let's get out of here."

As I grabbed my son and tried to get out of the restaurant without having any eye contact with the old man, Sammy was wriggling and leaned over me with his arms outstretched. All of a sudden Sammy propelled himself from my arms to his.

It all happened in a split second, and suddenly a very old man and a very young baby met. As Sammy put his head on the old man's ragged shoulder the man's eyes closed and tears welled around his lashes. His aged hands, full of grime and pain and hard labour, gently ever so gently cradled my baby. I was awestruck.

The old man rocked the baby back and forth, then opened both eyes and looked seriously into mine: "You take good care of this baby, now."

"I will," I muttered awkwardly.

He prised Sammy from his chest and placed him in my arms and addressed us: "God bless you, ma'am. You've given me my Christmas gift."

I think I muttered "Thanks."

With Sammy in my arms I ran for the car. My husband was wondering why I was crying and holding Sammy so tightly, and why I was saying "My God, please forgive me …"

> Christmas is most truly Christmas when we celebrate it by giving the light of love to those who need it most.
> Ruth Carter Stapleton

What to give this Christmas:

Your Time: Look for ways to help those who cannot help themselves

Your Love: Give love freely to those who need it most and deserve it least

Your Life: Your life was a gift to you from God; make it a gift from God to others

Your Lord: Jesus is the greatest gift of all. Introduce him to a friend.

Reach into your pocket;
reach into your heart
Christmas is the play; and
we all play a part

It is Christmas every time
you let God love others
through you ... every time
you smile at your brother
and offer him your hand.
Mother Teresa

Snowflakes softly falling
Upon your window they play;
Your blankets snug around you,
Into sleep you drift away.

I bend to gently kiss you,
when I see that on the floor
there's a letter, neatly written,
I wonder who it's for.

I quietly unfold it,
making sure you're still asleep;
It's a Christmas list for Santa
one my heart will always keep.

It started just as always
with the toys seen on TV,
A new watch for your father
and a winter coat for me.

But as my eyes read on
I could see that deep inside
there were many things you
    wished for
that your loving heart would hide.

You asked if your friend Molly
could have another dad;
It seems her father hits her
and it makes you very sad.

Then you asked dear Santa
if the neighbours down the street
could find a job, that they might
    have
some food, and clothes, and heat.

You saw a family on the news
whose house had blown away,

"Dear Santa, send them just one
    thing,
a place where they can stay."

"And Santa, those four biscuits
    that
I left you for a treat,
Could you take them to the
    children
who have nothing else to eat?"

"Do you know that little bear I
    have
the one I love so dear?
I'm leaving it for you to take
to Africa this year."

"And as you fly your reindeer
on this night of Jesus' birth,
Could your magic bring to
    everyone
goodwill and peace on earth."

"There's one last thing before you
    go:
so grateful I would be,
If you'd smile at Baby Jesus
in the manger by our tree."

I pulled the letter close to me,
I felt it melt my heart.
Those tiny hands had written
what no other could impart.

"And a little child shall lead them,"
was whispered in my ear
As I watched you sleep on
    Christmas Eve
while Santa Claus was here.

Come, let us all unite to sing:
God is love!
Let Heav'n and earth their praises bring,
God is love!
Let every soul from sin awake,
Let every heart sweet music make,
And sing with us for Jesus' sake:
God is love!

V is for Visits

So the Word became human and lived here on earth among us. He was full of unfailing love and faithfulness. And we have seen his glory, the glory of the only Son of the Father. (John 1:14)

Christmas is a time when we visit family and friends, and when we ourselves receive visitors. When someone makes the effort to travel a long way in order to be with us then the visit is all the more meaningful, as long of course as the visitor is a welcome guest. The great and startling truth about Christmas is that God in Christ chose to make an extraordinary journey from heaven to earth in order to visit us. Many people failed to welcome this divine visitor, this stranger from heaven. Some, however, recognised the importance of this visit and paid due homage. Some shepherds on the hills outside Jerusalem and some eastern astrologers from Persia visited the Visitor.

We are the
Visited Planet.
J B Phillips

God
often visits
us, but most of
the time we're not
at home.
French proverb

If our greatest need had been information,
God would have sent us an educator;

If our greatest need had been technology,
God would have sent us a scientist;

If our greatest need had been money,
God would have sent us an economist;

If our greatest need had been pleasure,
God would have sent us an entertainer;

But our greatest need was forgiveness,
so God sent us a Saviour.

A man sent his elderly parents a microwave oven one Christmas. Here's how he recalls the experience:

"They were excited that now they, too, could be a part of the instant generation. When Dad unpacked the microwave and plugged it in, literally within seconds the microwave transformed two smiles into a frown! Even after reading the directions, they couldn't make it work.

Two days later, my mother was playing bridge with a friend and confessed her inability to get that microwave oven even to boil water.

'To get this darn thing to work,' she exclaimed, 'I really don't need better directions; I just needed my son to bring the gift in person!'"

When God gave the gift of salvation, he didn't send a booklet of complicated instructions for us to figure out; he sent his Son.

One of my favourite stories is about a missionary teaching in Africa. Before Christmas, he had been telling his native students how Christians, as an expression of their joy, gave each other presents on Christ's birthday.

On Christmas morning, one of the natives brought the missionary a seashell of lustrous beauty. When asked where he had discovered such an extraordinary shell, the native said he had walked many miles to a certain bay, the only spot where such shells could be found.

"I think it was wonderful of you to travel so far to get this lovely gift for me," the teacher exclaimed.

His eyes brightening, the native replied, "Long walk, part of gift."

A housewife was one day washing dishes in the kitchen sink after the children had left for school. She looked at one particular plate. She stared at it for a long time and asked over and over again, "How many times have I washed this plate? How many times have I dried it? How many times will I wash it and dry it again?" She then set down the plate, took off her apron, packed a few of her belongings, and left.

That night she called home to tell her husband that she was all right, but that she just could not come home again. From time to time, over the next several weeks, she would call just to see how her husband and children were doing. But she would never tell them where she was, or accede to the pleas from her family to return.

The husband hired a detective to search for her and, after picking up a few leads, the detective tracked her down. She was in another state, living upstairs in a small apartment over a luncheonette where she had a job as a waitress. Her husband set out immediately to bring her home. When he found the place where she was staying, he knocked on the door of her upstairs apartment. She opened the door, saw him, and did not say a word. She went to her bedroom, packed her belongings, and silently followed him out to the car. Then, in silence, he drove her back home.

Several hours later when the two of them were alone in their bedroom he finally spoke, and he asked her, "Why didn't you come home before? Over the phone I begged you to return. Why didn't you come?"

The wife answered, "I heard your words, but it wasn't until you came for me that I realised how much you cared and how important I was to you."

God from on high hath heard;
Let sighs and sorrows cease;
Lo! from the opening Heav'n descends
To man the promised Peace.

W is for Wonder

Jesus called a small child over to him and put the child among them. Then he said, "I assure you, unless you turn from your sins and become as little children, you will never get into the Kingdom of Heaven. Therefore, anyone who becomes as humble as this little child is the greatest in the Kingdom of Heaven." (Matthew 18:2–4)

Laura Wilder has made the observation that "our hearts grow tender with childhood memories and love of kindred, and we are better throughout the year for having in spirit become a child again at Christmas time". Christmas reminds us of the importance of the gift of wonder. Jesus said that only those who become like little children can enter the Kingdom of God. Similarly, only those who approach the real meaning of Christmas with childlike wonder will discover the reason for this season.

There's nothing sadder in this world than to awake Christmas morning and not be a child.

Erma Bombeck

Each year, God asks us to shed one more coat of awareness, one more dream state, and come alive to the vision of God's plan for each of us and the world at large.

The older we get, the harder this is to do. As children we had a sense of wonder. Our eyes were wide open and drinking in the fascinating gifts we beheld … Our thirsty souls could not have enough of the wonders of creation. Then, somehow, we grew too old to dream. We tired of the abundance of the world, or at least grew weary of keeping up with the feast of life, and stepped away from the banquet of life. The natural gift of wonder God gave us as children was meant to be kept alive … Instead we let wonder go to sleep.

Revd Alfred McBride

Elizabeth Barrett Browning, the 19th-century poet, wrote: "Earth's crammed with heaven, and every common bush afire with God; And only he who sees takes off his shoes."

Unless we open our eyes to the wonders of God, no revelation takes place, and our world sits and waits for miracles while the wonders of God dance all around us. Let's open our eyes and ears to the glory of God, the God who comes to us in the majesty of creation, the Lord of the universe who meets us in the child of Bethlehem.

Christmas is for children. But it is for grown-ups too. Even if it is a headache, a chore, and nightmare, it is a period of necessary defrosting of chill and hidebound hearts.
Lenora Mattingly Weber

The way to Christmas lies through an ancient gate … It is a little gate, child-high, child-wide, and there is a password: "Peace on earth to men of goodwill". May you, this Christmas, become as a little child again and enter into his Kingdom.
Angelo Patri

The wonderment in a small child's eyes,
The ageless awe in the Christmas skies,
The nameless joy that fills the air,
The throngs that kneel in praise and prayer ...
These are the things that make us know
That men may come and men may go,
But none will ever find a way
To banish Christ from Christmas Day,
For with each child there's born again
A mystery that baffles men.

Helen Steiner Rice

Christmas! The very word brings joy to our hearts. No matter how we may dread the rush, the long Christmas lists for gifts and cards to be bought and given – when Christmas Day comes there is still the same warm feeling we had as children, the same warmth that enfolds our hearts and our homes.

Joan Winmill Brown

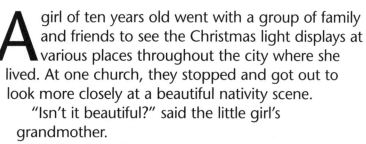

A girl of ten years old went with a group of family and friends to see the Christmas light displays at various places throughout the city where she lived. At one church, they stopped and got out to look more closely at a beautiful nativity scene.

"Isn't it beautiful?" said the little girl's grandmother.

"Look at all the animals, and Mary, Joseph and the baby Jesus."

"Yes, Grandma," replied the girl. "It's really nice. But one thing bothers me. Isn't baby Jesus ever going to grow up? He's the same size he was last year!"

This is Christmas: not the tinsel, not the giving and receiving, not even the carols, but the humble heart that receives anew the wondrous gift, the Christ.

Frank McKibben

We have become so accustomed to the idea of divine love and of God's coming at Christmas that we no longer feel the shiver of fear that God's coming should arouse in us.
Dietrich Bonhoeffer

Was there a moment, known only to God, when all the stars held their breath, when the galaxies paused in their dance for a fraction of a second, and the Word, who had called it all into being, went with all His love into the womb of a young girl?
Madeleine L'Engle

Nothing's as mean as giving a little child something useful for Christmas.
Kin Hubbard

Christmas demands faith, because Christmas is a mystery. Our reason cannot succeed in trying to understand how God could possibly have loved us to such degree. The shepherds are given a sign. They will find him in a manger. There the infant Jesus has been placed ... a sign of extreme poverty and of God's supreme humility. Such a thing baffles the intellect. It teaches us that to welcome the message of Christ, the divine Redeemer, reason must be laid aside. Only humility, which melts into trust and adoration, can comprehend and welcome God's saving humility.

Pope John Paul II

Whatever else be lost among the years,
Let us keep Christmas still a shining thing;
Whatever doubts assail us, or what fears,
Let us hold close one day, remembering
Its poignant meaning for the hearts of men,
Let us get back our childlike faith again.

Grace Noll Crowell

If, for us, reality is material only; if we gaze at the birth (of Jesus) with the modern eye which acknowledges nothing spiritual, sees nothing divine, demands the hard facts only ... if truth for us is merely empirical, then we are left with a photograph of small significance: a derelict husband, an immodest mother, a baby cradled in a feed trough in an outdoor shelter for pack animals ... But those for whom this is the only way to gaze at Christmas must themselves live lives bereft of meaning: nothing spiritual, nothing divine, no awe, never a gasp of adoration, never the sense of personal humiliation before glory nor the shock of personal exaltation when glory chooses also to bow down and to love.

Walter Wangerin

God revels in dissonance – in putting together things that have never been put together before. A Saviour during the census. The singing of angels in fugue with shepherds' earthy stories. The eternal Word wrapped in baby clothes.

Barbara K Lundblad

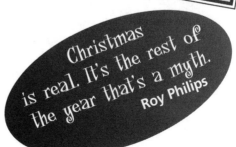

Christmas is real. It's the rest of the year that's a myth.
Roy Philips

It is good to be children sometimes, and never better than at Christmas, when its mighty Founder was a child himself.
Charles Dickens

Welcome all wonders in one sight!
Eternity shut in a span!
Summer in winter, day in night,
Heaven in earth, and God in man.
Great little one! Whose lowly birth
Lifts earth to heav'n, stoops heav'n to earth.
Richard Crashaw

To travel the road to Bethlehem
Is to keep a rendezvous with wonder
To answer the call of wisdom
And to bow the knee in worship.
John Knight

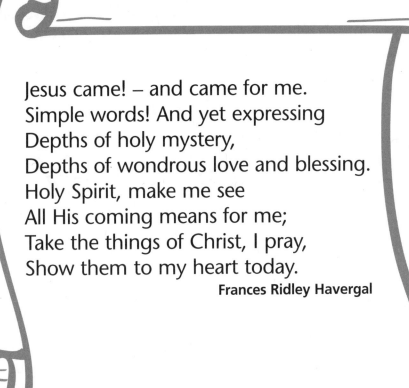

Jesus came! – and came for me.
Simple words! And yet expressing
Depths of holy mystery,
Depths of wondrous love and blessing.
Holy Spirit, make me see
All His coming means for me;
Take the things of Christ, I pray,
Show them to my heart today.

Frances Ridley Havergal

X is for Xmas

But although the world was made through Jesus Christ, the world didn't recognise him when he came. Even in his own land and among his own people, he was not accepted. (John 1:10–11)

Many people miss the real meaning of Christmas and one of the clearest indications of this is the way the word "Christmas" is being replaced by the shorthand "Xmas". This shows how many of us are taking the Christ out of Christmas. This of course is nothing new. Right from the very beginning people have missed the real meaning of this season. When Jesus was born, most people missed his birth and missed the significance of the most momentous event in history. For the last two thousand years people have been celebrating Xmas rather than Christmas. But, as my friend Paul Wilson has said, if you take the Christ out of Christmas, all you're left with is M & S!

Ten Commandments for Christmas

1. You shall not leave "Christ" out of Christmas, making it "Xmas". To some, "X" is unknown.

2. You shall prepare your soul for Christmas. Spend not so much on gifts that your soul is forgotten.

3. You shall not let Santa Claus replace Christ, thus robbing the day of its spiritual reality.

4. You shall not burden the shop girl, the mailman, and the merchant with complaints and demands.

5. You shall give yourself with your gift. This will increase its value a hundredfold, and the one who receives it shall treasure it for ever.

6. You shall not value gifts received by their cost. Even the least expensive may signify love, and that is more priceless than silver and gold.

7. You shall not neglect the needy. Share your blessings with many who will go hungry and cold if you are not generous.

8. You shall not neglect your church. Its services highlight the true meaning of the season.

9. You shall be as a little child. Not until you become in spirit as a little one are you ready to enter into the kingdom of Heaven.

10. You shall give your heart to Christ. Let Him be at the top of your Christmas list.

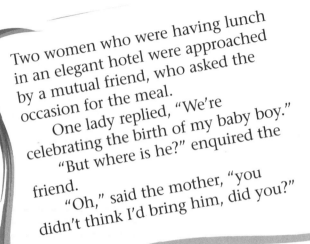

Two women who were having lunch in an elegant hotel were approached by a mutual friend, who asked the occasion for the meal.

One lady replied, "We're celebrating the birth of my baby boy."

"But where is he?" enquired the friend.

"Oh," said the mother, "you didn't think I'd bring him, did you?"

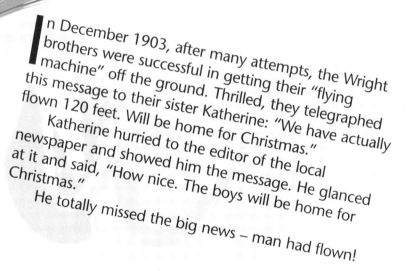

In December 1903, after many attempts, the Wright brothers were successful in getting their "flying machine" off the ground. Thrilled, they telegraphed this message to their sister Katherine: "We have actually flown 120 feet. Will be home for Christmas." Katherine hurried to the editor of the local newspaper and showed him the message. He glanced at it and said, "How nice. The boys will be home for Christmas."

He totally missed the big news – man had flown!

Many people think that it's wrong to call Christmas "Xmas". "It's like taking Christ away from Christmas!" they say. It's a reflection of the way Christmas has become separated from the birthday of Jesus Christ. But let's think about it in another way. When I receive a letter with a row of Xs at the bottom, it tells me that the sender loves me very much. When we see Christmas written "Xmas" it can remind us that God loves us so much that he sent his own Son to tell us. So Xmas starts with a big kiss to remind us of God's great love. And of course an X is a cross and Jesus' love took him all the way from the stable to the cross.

Judith Merrell

THEY MISSED HIM! They were looking for a lion, He came as a Lamb, and they missed Him.

They were looking for a warrior, He came as a Peacemaker, and they missed Him.

They were looking for a king, He came as a Servant, and they missed Him.

They were looking for liberation from Rome, He submitted to the Roman stake, and they missed Him.

They were looking for a fit to their mould, He was the mould-breaker, and they missed Him.

Will you?

In my lifetime, the Christmas card has changed. Am I alone in noticing the marginalisation if not elimination of virtually any references to what the festival marks, the birth of the Christ child? ... Clinton Cards, with 700 stores the largest specialist retailer, admitted that out of 960 cards in its smaller shops, just three refer to the religious significance of the season.

Sir Roy Strong, Christmas 2002

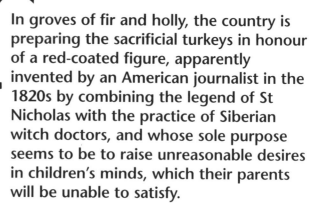

In groves of fir and holly, the country is preparing the sacrificial turkeys in honour of a red-coated figure, apparently invented by an American journalist in the 1820s by combining the legend of St Nicholas with the practice of Siberian witch doctors, and whose sole purpose seems to be to raise unreasonable desires in children's minds, which their parents will be unable to satisfy.

Meanwhile, some of us will be celebrating Christmas.

The story of a little boy at school defines for us how we have secularised Christmas. A teacher had asked the class to construct a manger scene in the corner of the classroom.

They built the stable, covered the floor with hay, and filled the structure with the figures of Mary, Joseph, the shepherds, the wise men, the animals, and a tiny doll, representing the baby Jesus.

All the children were excited about the project except one little boy, who kept looking at the manger scene with a troubled expression.

The teacher finally asked him if something was wrong.

With childlike wisdom, the boy said:

"What I'd like to know is, where does God fit in?"

Missing the significance of a child's birth is nothing new. History is full of examples of this kind of thing.

Take 1809. The big news was Napoleon's bloody military victories against Austria and then, in the Peninsular War, against Spain. These battles filled the front pages.

But the birth columns for that year might have shown the following names:

William Gladstone, who became one of England's finest statesmen.

Alfred Tennyson, who would one day become a great poet.

Edgar Allan Poe, who became one of America's greatest writers of fiction.

Charles Darwin, who would become the world's most influential scientist.

And, in a rugged log cabin in Hardin County, Kentucky, Abraham Lincoln.

The newspapers of the day were full of reports about Napoleon's battles. But history was really being shaped not on the battlefields of Europe but in the cradles of England and America.

In the same way, the news two thousand years ago was about Rome, and particularly the census edict from Augustus. But world history was being shaped in a manger in Bethlehem, and only a few shepherds and some wealthy Arabs saw it.

Adapted from Chuck Swindoll

A week after the terrible events of September 11th, a CNN reporter was at Ground Zero at the site of the Twin Towers in New York. There were ruins everywhere.

As the camera panned round the ruins, it lingered on a room a few storeys up where the floor was still intact. Only one wall remained. On that wall hung a picture of Jesus.

As the reporter saw it, he was stunned. "My goodness," he stuttered. "No need for words there." And the camera remained for some time without commentary on the portrait of the Son of God.

You could so easily have missed it. But it was there. The Rescuer was in the Rubble. Not where you would have expected, perhaps. But he was there.

Take Christ out of Christmas and December becomes the bleakest and most colourless month of the year.

Christmas is the gift from heaven
Of God's Son given for free
If Christmas isn't found in your heart
You won't find it under a tree

C is for the Christ-child, a child of love and light
H is for the Heavens that were bright that holy night
R is for the Radiance of the star that led the way
I is for the lowly Inn where the infant Jesus lay
S is for the Shepherds who beheld the Christmas star
T is for the Tidings the angels told afar
M is for the Magi with their gifts of myrrh and gold
A is for the Angels who were awesome to behold
S is for the Saviour who was born to save all men

And together this spells CHRISTMAS,
Which we celebrate again.

Helen Steiner Rice

A 1999 survey by television company OnDigital has found that, among the under-30s, people know more about Christmas television programmes than they do about Christmas itself.

In the survey, only 28% of the age group could name the three gifts brought by the Wise Men to Jesus, and only one in five knew that the king who ordered the killing of the firstborn was called Herod.

In contrast, 64% knew that the television detective who drove a red Jaguar was called Morse.

What child is this, who, laid to rest
On Mary's lap, is sleeping?
Whom angels greet with anthems sweet,
While shepherds watch are keeping?
This, this is Christ the King,
Whom shepherds guard and angels sing: Haste, haste to bring him laud,
The Babe, the Son of Mary!

Y is for Yule

In the beginning the Word already existed. He was with God, and he was God. He was in the beginning with God. He created everything there is. Nothing exists that he didn't make. Life itself was in him, and this life gives light to everyone. The light shines through the darkness, and the darkness can never extinguish it. (John 1:1–5)

The origins of Christmas are ancient and complex. In antiquity the winter solstice was celebrated on the 25th of December as the "birthday of the Unconquered Sun". It was in the fourth century that Christianity assigned the birth of Christ to that date. The revamped festival soon absorbed influences from other sources, including those of the Nordic midwinter feast of "Yule".

The pagans of northern Europe celebrated their own winter solstice, known as Yule. The word Yule itself means "wheel", the wheel being a pagan symbol for the sun. Yule was symbolic of the pagan sun god, Mithras. The birth of Mithras was observed on the shortest day of the year. It was customary to light a candle to encourage Mithras, and the sun, to reappear next year.

The custom of burning the Yule log goes back to the Middle Ages. It was originally a Nordic tradition. The Yule log was actually a whole tree that was selected with great care and brought into the home with great ceremony. The largest end of the log would be placed in the fireplace while the rest of the tree stuck out into the room! The log would be lit from the remains of the previous year's log, which had been carefully stored away.

Many pre-Christian myths and festivals anticipate the birth of Jesus Christ. Sometimes people claim that Christianity is simply a new myth that was created out of existing myths. But the truth is that the birth of Jesus was a historical fact. The evidence for Jesus of Nazareth is greater than for any other figure in the ancient world. Far from Christianity being another myth, it is in reality what C S Lewis called "myth become fact". It is the myths of dying and rising gods become actual fact in history. Many of the myths of ancient and indeed existing cultures are actually anticipations of what was to come in the life and death of an actual human being, Jesus of Nazareth. They are examples of the light that enlightens every human being and anticipations of the true light revealed in Jesus (John 1:4).

In 1962, a missionary couple called Don and Carol Richardson went to minister to the Sawi people in New Guinea. The Sawi were head-hunting cannibals!

Two rival tribes of the Sawi people were at loggerheads with each other. After a long and sustained period of violence and bloodshed between these two tribes, the Richardsons decided to leave. They simply couldn't find any point of contact with them. However, the Sawi begged them to stay, saying, "If you'll stay, we promise we'll make peace in the morning."

The next morning the two tribes lined up on either side of a clearing. A man dashed into his hut, grabbed his newborn son, and began to run towards the other tribe. His face was full of agony. His wife ran after him, screaming.

But the man – her husband – didn't stop. He ran to the other tribe and presented the boy to them.

"Plead the peace child for me. I give you my son, and I give you my name," he said.

Moments later, someone from that tribe performed the same agonising sacrifice with the same intensity and passion.

Later the Richardsons discovered that, as long as those two children remained alive, the tribes were bound to peace. If they died, then war would break out.

As the Richardsons witnessed all this, Don realised that this was the point of contact he was looking for. The next time he spoke to the Sawi he told them of the perfect Peace Child, Jesus. Eventually, many of the Sawi became followers of Christ.

Several years later, on Christmas Day, hundreds of Sawi from every tribe – tribes that had fought each other for years – gathered together for a feast for the first time.

A Sawi preacher stood up and read in his own language a scripture that few people in the history of the world have ever understood so clearly:

Unto us a child is born, unto us a son is given, and the government shall be upon His shoulders, and He shall be called Wonderful Counsellor, Mighty God, Everlasting Father, Prince of Peace.

Later, the Richardsons wrote that it was the best Christmas of their lives.

See the blazing Yule before us,
Fa la la la la, la la la la.
Strike the harp and join the chorus,
Fa la la la la, la la la la.

Follow me in merry measure,
Fa la la, la la la, la la la.
While I tell of Yuletide treasure,
Fa la la la la, la la la la.

Z is for ZZZZZZZZZZZZZZZZZZZZZZZZZ

I will lie down in peace and sleep,
for you alone, O LORD, will keep me safe.
(Psalm 4:8)

The festivities of Christmas end with the sigh of contentment and the sound of snoring. Exhausted parents get to bed having spent the whole day orchestrating the opening of presents, the visit to church, the Christmas dinner, the clearing-up operation and many other things besides. Christmas is a public holiday designed to help us take a much-needed rest. But the irony of it all is that we often end up doing more on Christmas Day, and becoming more exhausted, than on any normal working day. Consequently, when adults eventually lay their heads upon their pillows, they can often feel more tired than at any other time of the year!

And there were in the country children keeping watch over their stockings by the fireplace. And lo! Santa Claus came upon them; and they were so afraid. And Santa said unto them: "Fear not, for behold I bring you good tidings of great joy which will be to all people who can afford them. For unto you will be given great feasts of turkey, stuffing and pudding and many presents, and this shall be a sign unto you; ye shall find the presents, wrapped in bright paper, lying beneath a tree adorned with tinsel, coloured balls and lights. And suddenly there will be with you a multitude of relatives and friends, praising you and saying, 'Thank you so much, it was just what I wanted'. And it shall come to pass as the friends and relatives have gone away into their own homes, the parents shall say to one another, 'What a mess to clear up! I'm tired, let's go to bed and pick it up tomorrow. Thank goodness Christmas only comes once a year!' "

God grant you the light in Christmas, which is faith,
The warmth of Christmas, which is love,
The radiance of Christmas, which is purity,
The righteousness of Christmas, which is justice,
The belief in Christmas, which is truth,
The all of Christmas, which is Christ.

Wilda English

May the Babe of Bethlehem be yours to tend
May the Boy of Nazareth be yours for friend
May the Man of Galilee his healing send
May the Christ of Calvary his courage lend
May the risen Lord his presence send
And his holy angels defend you to the end.

Pilgrim's Prayer

A Christmas Prayer
by Robert Louis Stevenson

Loving Father,
help us remember the birth of Jesus,
that we may share in the song of the angels,
the gladness of the shepherds,
and worship of the wise men.
Close the door of hate
and open the door of love all over the world.
Let kindness come with every gift
and good desires with every greeting.
Deliver us from evil by the blessing
which Christ brings,
and teach us to be merry with clear hearts.
May the Christmas morning
make us happy to be thy children,
and Christmas evening bring us to our beds
with grateful thoughts,
forgiving and forgiven,
for Jesus' sake.

Amen.

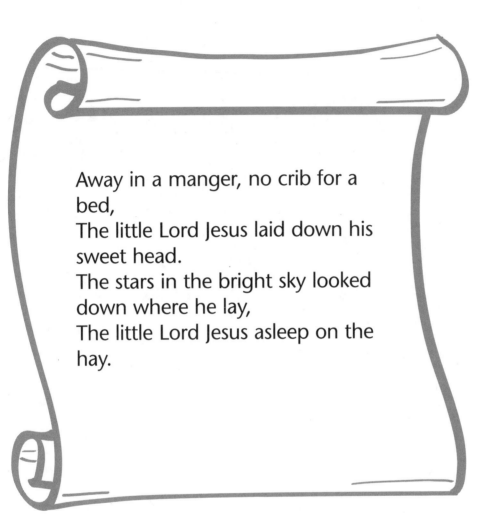

Away in a manger, no crib for a
bed,
The little Lord Jesus laid down his
sweet head.
The stars in the bright sky looked
down where he lay,
The little Lord Jesus asleep on the
hay.

A Stocking Full of Christmas